YOU'RE NOT OLD UNTIL YOU'RE NINETY:

Best to Be Prepared, However

ℐ

REBECCA LATIMER

Blue Dolphin Publishing
1997

Published by Blue Dolphin Publishing, Inc.
P.O. Box 8, Nevada City, CA 95959
Orders: 1-800-643-0765

ISBN: 1-57733-009-9

Library of Congress Cataloging-in-Publication Data

Latimer, Rebecca H.
   You're not old until you're ninety : best to prepared,
however / Rebecca Latimer
      p.   cm.
   Includes bibliographical references.
   ISBN 1-57733-009-9
   1. Aged—Life skills guides.   2. Aging—Psychological
aspects.   3. Old age.   I. Title
HQ1061.L358   1997
646.7'0084'6—dc21   97-6720
                                                    CIP

Cover photo of East Hill near Calais, Vermont
by Frederick P. Latimer.
Cover design by Lito Castro

Printed in Canada by Best Book Manufacturers

5   4   3   2   1

YOU'RE NOT OLD UNTIL

YOU'RE NINETY

Dedication

I wish to thank my husband, Fred, and our two sons, Doug and John, for their wholehearted support through the months it took me to write this book and see it through to publication.

I am also deeply indebted (literally!) to the Thanks Be to Grandmother Winifred Foundation for the astonishing grant they gave me, as well as their sincere and continuing interest in my well-being.

I am especially fortunate in having so many friends who contributed encouragement, affection, and precious time to my project. I am truly sorry I can't list all their names, but I must especially thank those of them who helped me over rough spots, often at considerable sacrifice to their other obligations.

Rebecca

ℒ

Table of Contents

∅

CHAPTER ONE

The Beginning

I MUST TELL YOU AT ONCE that I have become over ninety in the course of writing this book, and yes, being over ninety is different. Nevertheless, though I keep hearing sarcastic references to The Golden Years, I can't quite agree with that dismal view of old age. I have been luckier than most. I have found that I can meet the challenges and changes that come with age without too much difficulty. For various reasons, I can say with all honesty, I'd rather be a very old woman than a very young one. It is true that I have lost my physical resilience, but new friends and interests outweigh my losses. Yes, I'd rather be over seventy than under fifty.

Whatever age you may be now, even if your life has been joyous all the way, or at least satisfactory, you will find it worthwhile to consider the path laid out in this book; it will help you handle the changes that lie before you.

I might not have questioned why my old age has turned out to be as it has if four younger friends, Cynthia,

Christie, Pam and Sue, hadn't inquired about it. They asked me (separately since they don't know each other) "You are still enjoying life, you are still writing, you laugh a lot! How have you managed this? What is your secret?" So I too began to wonder how this had happened.

I have been keeping journals ever since my childhood. My first notebook is dated 1914 and the latest is my present one. The bulk of them cover the twenty-five years I lived in Europe, the Middle East and Central America. They will end, I think, in California where I now live. These journals make a long uneven line on the shelf of the bookcase just across from my typewriter; they cover my entire life. Thinking about my "secret," I knew the key to this puzzle must lie somewhere in those pages.

There was, however, a formidable obstacle to taking up this challenge. Being a writer, I knew I would have to write the story, if I found one. I knew that my metamorphosis must have taken years, nor could it have taken place simply because my diplomat-husband had exchanged his top hat for a mortarboard by becoming a professor. I also knew that the story would not make for light reading. It would have to be a serious book.

But my husband, to whom I've now been married nearer seventy than sixty years, had had a stroke and I was taking care of him. I saw no prospect of being able to find the time and energy to give to writing a book. The night I came to this unhappy conclusion, I had a dream. I wrote it down in the morning.

We had moved into a small house in a new development. Our house had no room that I could use for writing, though I had hoped to find a small nook where I could write at least one day a week. I walked outside to survey our neighbors. Their houses were exactly like mine and I knew they wouldn't have any extra space either.

I left the little cluster of new houses and found myself on a wide, dirt road where nothing had disturbed its slightly dusty surface. I walked lightly down it. A beautiful golden light lay on the fields and distant hills. It was as if I were in a foreign country.

On the right side of the road I saw a strong, waist-high stone wall, broad and solid. Behind it I could see a grove of low trees with gnarled trunks and shiny leaves on spreading branches. "Old olive trees," I thought.

I came to a wide opening in the wall where the marks of narrow wheels on the thin grass showed carriages had often entered the little grove. Where the stone wall met the entrance, a sign had been propped up on it. It said LIBRARY! As if drawn by a magnet, I turned and walked through the entrance. Under the shady branches of the old trees, I saw a small one-story building with a red tiled roof. A sign over the wooden door said LIBRERIA DE SEÑOR DON OLIVEROS & CASTILLA-NOS. I wondered who this gentleman was. The sign said in small letters that it was open one day a week. I saw the door was ajar so I pushed it open and walked in.

A thin, pale young man was sitting at a desk in a corner of the room. Yes, he told me, I would be welcome. I would be given a table at which I could work. I could work all day, one day a week.

When I woke from this dream I knew I would be able to find a way to write this book. It turned out that the dream was not only prophetic but practical, because the next day I noticed a small advertisement in the magazine *Poets and Writers*. Its headline asked, "Are you over 54?" I could truthfully answer, "Yes, I am!" The Thanks Be to Grandmother Winifred Foundation which had run the ad was ready to encourage and even fund older women who had worthwhile projects, so I wrote them. The women who run the foundation became my friends at once—and

4 YOU'RE NOT OLD UNTIL YOU'RE NINETY

still are. I was awarded enough money to get started on this book. With part-time help installed, I went to work.

Before I began writing, however, I wrote to Christie, Cynthia, Sue, and Pam. I told them I was going to try to find out how it had happened that, in my old age, I was enjoying life more than ever before. I added that, if they followed my path, I couldn't promise them they wouldn't have any of the physical troubles of old age because I haven't avoided arthritis and glaucoma. Nor could I promise them they would escape tragedy because that has come my way, too. But I have discovered to my astonishment that I can handle whatever comes, even handle it calmly and for me that's reward enough for the intermittent work I have done. (May you be as lucky!)

I promised them, however, I would tell them exactly what I did and what I learned. "You'll be surprised," I added. "I have done things you may well find impossible to believe."

I hope you won't decide at this point that you can't take this book seriously because either you are too young or too old, or too lazy, or too busy. Even if you follow its advice halfheartedly, using only your left hand, you will find it has made a difference.

I will add, too, please don't be put off by the fact it was young women who asked for this book. As you will read later, my friend, Reg Robinson, has asked for it, too. It's written really for anyone, man or woman, who hopes to enjoy old age.

∅

CHAPTER TWO

Moving Forward

THIS BOOK IS NOT GOING TO BE AN EXACT GUIDE with maps and timetables and the cost of every item. It simply relates, with the help of the journals I've kept through the years, my gradual progress toward an understanding of what we are offered when we are given the gift of life and how we can take advantage of it. The surprise for me was finding there is general agreement about this on the part of such disparate thinkers as Gurdjieff, Alan Watts, Elmer and Alyce Green and Carlos Castaneda. Going even further back, Jesus, the Buddha and Mohammed were all actually headed in the same direction; only the details varied.

What they all realized was that most of us live our entire lives without ever really waking up. We just float along on the surface of life, pushed by the minutiae of the daily demands on us, though a few do break away at some point in the blind journey, stopping to wonder where we all are going.

To explain to you the path I embarked on when I began to wake up, I will have to tell you how things were with me before that, and also what began to awaken me. I hope you will be able to glean enough information from my experience to chart your own course with some confidence.

Until the late 1960s, when my husband and I moved into a small redwood house in the woods in Antrim, New Hampshire, I had been too busy to stop to listen to the small voice inside me I had heard from time to time, asking me a question. I had recently turned sixty.

I must tell you too that I have not yet gotten the final answer to my confused question, which I began to hear clearly, "Isn't there more than this? In myself? In the world?" I have, however, acquired enough understanding to have changed me from the self-conscious, inhibited, nervous diplomatic wife I had been to a different person. I am now able to enjoy the people I meet and the things I am doing, free to express my opinion and even act on it.

I hadn't actually put this into words until my four friends had questioned me. It had been a gradual process. I had not found a guru. I had simply studied the books I had available and tried to apply their advice. I had thought, at first, as you probably have thought too, that I would find a simple formula that I could apply fairly easily, but instead I found I would have to work. I was helped in that work by various exercises and suggestions that strengthened my self-discipline and changed my old, rigid attitudes, but all this involved work.

Now that you are warned that it is not an easy path, I am going to lay it out for you. I will go ahead and tell you my story. As you may already have realized, the first condition for answering the question, "How can I get the most out of the years now left to me?" is to find time to be alone in a quiet room where you can hear the answer. For me this happened in New Hampshire when, for the first time since I was born, I was alone all day. My husband was away teaching at the nearby college and both our sons were grown and on their own.

I loved the solitude. I'm sure that was a help. A distracted mind is so preoccupied with its own problems that it can't hear that quiet voice. I felt very comfortable to be living in that little house perched on a slope in a clearing surrounded by woods. It was as though we were living in the center of a forest whose inhabitants—the birds, squirrels and chipmunks—quickly accepted us. The stone ledge that topped the retaining wall above the driveway became a perfect feeding station for the chipmunks. Before long they were eating from my hand. A mother squirrel regularly summoned me to feed her by jumping on the ladder leaning against the house. When I heard the telltale rattle, I would run out to the sundeck to find her sitting on the railing, her tiny pink nipples, a double row of buttons, prominent on her pale, furry breast.

An early entry in my journal says it all: *Is it living here in this quiet little house in the woods, watching the seasons swing past me faster and faster, that has suddenly made me know in my bones that I am mortal? Today I have been wondering how much more time I have. I've never thought about it before. It didn't seem to be important. I knew I had plenty of time! But today I realize I am sixty-three. Do I have ten years? That's not very long! Twenty? That's better. I could get a lot of books written in twenty years.*

But now I think of my mother. Will I be able to write books in my eighties? My mother is nearly one hundred, but these last years she has lost touch with reality, poor woman. And she is blind. Will I inherit this blindness? I can't know.

I don't think I realized then how handicapped I was, though I can see it clearly from this distance. I thought only that I wanted to make the most of the time I had left, but if we think of our starting point as zero, then I was at minus zero. I was loaded down with inhibitions, fears and a feeling of inadequacy that I had acquired when I had been the shy, plain young woman who had hoped to go to college. Instead, I finished high school—and my education—at sixteen, having had only five years of formal education.

My inner feeling that I didn't measure up to accepted standards was then intensified and magnified by twenty-five years in the stifling atmosphere of the diplomatic service, where I was an unhappy misfit as the wife of an American Foreign Service officer. (Luckily, he didn't see me that way.) But the diplomatic service was finally behind me when we settled into that quiet little house in the woods.

To add to my feeling of peace, it snows a lot in New Hampshire. The long winters only intensified my feeling of being out of the "real" world.

Our front door, at the top of steps leading from the driveway, was a sliding glass panel. When the snow came, I looked out on the falling snow from our comfortable, warm living room. I described the scene over and over in my journal: *February 25, 1969. It began snowing yesterday morning. The snow piled along the roadside by the plow is already as high as the roofs of the passing cars. By afternoon the roads were slippery and choked with snow. Fred and I went out for a walk when the snow stopped for a little while in the late afternoon. It was a newly-made white world. No tracks anywhere but the long, slender leaf-like prints of our snowshoes. The lawn, covered with snow, is now level with the top of the front steps. The birds are crowding in to be fed. The chipmunks, of course, have been asleep in their burrows since the first real frost.*

There is nothing as heavenly as being snowed in. I know nobody will expect me to go anywhere. It's like being on an island. It's like being inside of one of those glass paperweights. It is peace.

Even without the snowstorms, I found myself in a perfect place to work. I had already improvised a small work room in the basement that I had made cheerful by stapling a colorful Turkish *kilim* to cover the heating pipes. I was writing a book for young people, but I was also reading and thinking. I had known for some time I was not at all the person I wanted to be, that I felt I might become. But how could I change? In my reading I had gathered that serious people felt that meditation was important and though I didn't know exactly how one meditated, I was sure that disciplining the mind was the first step, so I tried that.

When I hopefully set a timer for ten minutes and lay down on a cot, I found that my mind instantly began sending me a summons I couldn't ignore. It was reminding me that I had heard Alan Watts speak many years earlier in Salt Lake City. I jumped up to look for the Salt Lake journals. When I pulled out the right one, I found I had heard him speak in 1963 at the University of Utah. The journal entry transfixed me.

May 5, 1963: Last night Alan Watts spoke. He had a monkish look. Thick hair which he wore brushed straight forward to his forehead where it was cut in a straight line. It was a sleek, burnished cap.

I remembered him then. I remembered how I tried not to miss a word. But this was not what I was looking for. I kept reading.

Watts said two things that stay with me: Learning and perception with our conscious mind is like using a flashlight to see in an auditorium, while the power of the unconscious mind to learn, understand and illumine is like the auditorium lit by flood lights.

I remembered how that had hit me when I heard it, and it hit me again as I read the passage, but I was distressed because I didn't know how to get in touch with my unconscious.

I read further:

He spoke of understanding with our unconscious by switching off the mind. He said that if you wish to hit a mark with a bow and arrow (and he made a beautiful gesture of drawing an arrow) you have to let the arrow go unconsciously. If you say "Now! " with your mind, the moment has already fled. You can struggle and struggle and when you give up the struggle, it will come — or you can help it by quiet meditation. "Stop listening to yourself talk in your mind. Empty it of words."

"Thank you, Alan Watts!" I said. I reset the timer, lay down on the cot, and again tried to empty my mind.

I didn't know at the time how emptying my mind would put me in touch with my unconscious, but I trusted Alan Watts. A good while later I discovered my unconscious usually speaks to me at unexpected moments, while I am meditating, or when I wake in the morning. It gives me the answer to some problem or tells me how to smooth out a rough passage in my writing. I am always taken by surprise.

From then on I tried, for at least a few minutes of every day, to hold my mind still. I hoped to ignore the thoughts trying steadily to distract me. Sometimes I was successful.

Along with the conviction I must learn to control my mind was the feeling I must change in some way. I was making unhappy entries in my journal:

I have put myself down all my life. I accepted the limitations thrust upon me. I should have forced myself to learn to argue reasonably, for instance, and to write a well-thought-out letter to a senator, to read carefully so I could repeat the fact I had learned instead of fumbling, mumbling and, in the end, feeling like a fool.

Later: *Today, as we walked out to the car, why did I say,
"Fred, will you let me drive?" Let me drive! I need a Consciousness Raising Group!*

And then a long entry with the title, WOMEN'S LIB—
MINE. I'll give you an excerpt:

*I wish I had made myself learn about cars. I actually don't
see them. If someone drives by, Fred can tell the make, the model
and year of the car, while I may have noticed its color, but more
likely only that it was driven by a young man with longish hair
and a beautiful mustache, who had a girl with long, straight,
yellow hair sitting beside him.*

*I have been made to feel foolish, impractical, very feminine
and unworldly because I don't recognize cars. I have accepted
this judgment which confirms the fact that I am foolish.*

But now I was trying to accept my limitations and
perhaps learn how to grow out of some of them. I was
reading as well as "meditating." I went on from Alan
Watts to Aldous Huxley.

Huxley has been a beacon for me ever since. I loved his
Perennial Philosophy in which he demonstrated that all
religions have the same basic principles. That if you lived
according to the doctrines of your own religion it didn't
matter if you were a Christian, a Moslem or a Hindu. I had
always been made uncomfortable by my Sunday School
teacher who seemed to consider everyone not a Christian
was a heathen and therefore doomed. Aldous Huxley, by
agreeing with me, erased the slight residue of guilt that I
had harbored for years. I still love Aldous Huxley.

*Aldous Huxley makes me want to re-order my life. His
"Don't borrow trouble" makes me think I shouldn't dwell so
much on how difficult old age will be, nor expect to be incompetent in a short time. A more rational attitude would be to
recognize that my physical strength has gotten gradually less,
and that I should rest more and not demand so much of my body,
but my mind hasn't deteriorated yet. In fact, in some ways, I feel*

I am stretching it more than I ever have done. So I should not cloud my present days with foreboding about the future.

(I have to add that I have found that the more I ask of my body, the more it is willing to give, and now I don't spare it. My body is like my mind; they both need exercise.)

As time went on, it began to seem as if I were slowly changing. I had made an unhappy entry in my journal in 1969:

I am afraid of a good many things. I am thoroughly neurotic. I don't like to travel by myself. I can't. I don't know why. I think it's the inhuman mechanistic rituals of travel that frighten me. As if I were the slave of the air line, following its commands, and would be punished if I misunderstood its orders. I have no feeling that transportation is arranged for the convenience of the traveler. I often wonder if I would get used to traveling alone if I had to do a lot of it. Or am I too old?

And then a triumphant P.S. in November 1970: *I flew from Keene, NH without Fred to New York City and made out okay!*

In 1971 an even more triumphant entry:

It seems a very strange thing that I've gotten to sixty-five and just now see that I haven't used my mind properly.

I have let myself skim a book instead of reading it. I have allowed myself to ignore statistics; I've never tried to understand them. Any simple problem, like a broken gadget in the kitchen, a recipe that doesn't turn out the same way twice, the mechanism of the car—all are things I don't try to understand.

Cross out that "don't!" Make it DIDN'T! I've suddenly changed. I don't just accept an inconvenience. I put my mind on it and usually win out. I read books conscientiously. I am even more rational in my personal relationships.

Why did I have to wait sixty-five years?!

So things were getting better, but it turned out that though Antrim was a magical place, time didn't stand still as I wished it would. Instead it taught me an unexpected aspect of time that I hadn't known before—that as you get older, time goes faster.

Fred had had his sixty-fifth birthday the year after he began teaching at Nathaniel Hawthorne College in 1968, yet it was two years later before we faced up to the cold truth that he was going to have to retire from teaching in 1972. We suddenly (it seemed) had to decide where we wanted to settle down for our "old age." We didn't really put our minds on this looming problem because we were campaigning vigorously for McGovern for president in a town where Republicans were as thick as the black flies in a New Hampshire summer, but we stopped once in a while to consider the future. We finally decided to move to Bennington, Vermont.

We had one conversation about our situation in 1971:

Fred and I were talking about old age. We agreed that when you are young, you never think about being old. Then, as you begin your sixties, age colors everything. You have to plan for a future in which you know your physical strength will decrease. (Better a house with one floor than two.) Of course you have to plan to have less ability to earn money and there will be less to live on. And you have to admit that somewhere in the future even this limited way of life comes to an end. And, in fact, you should think how it would be if you lost your partner, though this turns out to be impossible; you can't do it.

(I am not sure now this is good advice. In California we moved into a house with only one floor and now I simply can't climb stairs. I am wondering, if we had chosen a two-story house, would I still be briskly climbing the stairs to go to bed?)

In 1973 it seems we didn't really believe that we were getting old because we rented a two-story house in Bennington, Vermont, but before I tell you about it, I must tell you why we chose Vermont.

In 1955 we had innocently rented a house for the summer in Maple Corner, Vermont, a small farming community ten miles north of Montpelier on the County Road. We had no idea that Vermont would bewitch us, but we instantly fell in love with the place and the people. The next year we moved up all our possessions into a small rented house and, after that, our year revolved around returning to Maple Corner for the summer, until we moved to New Hampshire.

Since in Antrim we had reluctantly become aware that before long we were going to be "old people," we resisted the pull to go back once again to Maple Corner. Instead we decided to settle in Bennington, hoping the winters in that "southern" town might be a little less severe than some we had seen the edges of in Maple Corner.

We will always remember Maple Corner gratefully, however, for the warm friendships we made there. I especially have reason to thank Maple Corner because it was there I came upon two women who illuminated for me the possibilities inherent in both an active life and in old age.

The first, Mary Austin, was not a Vermonter but I associate her with Maple Corner as if she was just one of the many gifts I was given there. Vermont holds wonderful small-town auctions and estate sales, and it was at one of those that I came upon a book by Mary Austin that has been a part of my life ever since. I am looking at my bookcase now and there it is, *Everyman's Genius*, standing with four other books of hers and two about her. Mary Austin persuaded me not to be afraid of being out of step with my friends; she made it clear that many people went through their lives with their heads down, seeing only the road they were taking, convinced it was the right road because so many people were on it. Mary Austin also showed me that we have powers of which I was totally unaware.

The other woman was Mrs. Wheelock, a Vermont woman who lived all alone on a remote farm in a small clearing on the edge of deep, dark woods.

Mrs. Wheelock showed me that an independent woman can handle her life, even though this includes all the physical obstacles that present themselves when a widow-woman is living the life of the early settlers. In addition, Mrs. Wheelock lived on what is known today as "the poverty level" but she herself didn't know that.

I'll tell you about these two women in the next chapter. There is a third, Emily Rockwood but she will have a chapter all to herself later on. (It was Emily Rockwood who made that challenging statement: "YOU'RE NOT OLD UNTIL YOU'RE NINETY; BEST TO BE PREPARED, HOWEVER.")

SUMMING UP: If you want to get started right away, the first step is to make room in your day to be by yourself, out of reach of your phone, for a quarter of an hour. The second step is to find a timer, setting it for fifteen minutes. Then sit quietly, with eyes closed, trying to stop the stubborn flow of thoughts into your mind.

☒

CHAPTER THREE

Two Role Models

I NEVER MET MARY AUSTIN—except through her books. Born in 1868, on the 9th of September—by what magic, on my very own birthday thirty-seven years before me—she died in 1934, when I happened to be living in Finland and hadn't even heard of her. But her books were enough. Mary Austin made me realize for the first time that the world is a marvelous place, that my daily routine of cooking, cleaning and doing the laundry was not the whole of life, that there were wider horizons beyond my familiar world.

Mary Austin made me think about those other worlds, the worlds within our world, of which I had till then been totally unconscious. She told me that everyone had the unusual powers that she had. I didn't quite believe her but it was a liberating idea just in itself. It gave me more self-confidence, making me feel less frightened of the future.

In 1958, when I finally discovered Mary Austin, I was only fifty-three, still unaware of what was ahead of me. As she was to help me learn, I had been nearly asleep my entire life.

I think of the way I found Mary Austin as pure serendipity, though Carl Jung would probably have given it the
name of synchronicity, and my friend, Lois, would say it
was simple magic. Probably all three of us would be right.
As for the basic cause of such happenings, I think it lies
in being open to whatever comes along, even though it
seems outrageous at the time. (You might remember this.)

As I said earlier, we were living in Maple Corner,
Vermont. It was August and my husband's sisters had
come to visit us. They always loved shopping and especially loved Vermont's colorful auctions. It was fun to
chauffeur them around. One day they wanted to go to an
estate sale forty miles away. When we got there they were
excited by the antiques, but I found a room piled with
books and magazines. It was magic, of course, that I
immediately discovered an old *National Geographic* (January, 1939,) the very issue that had a color shot of me (yes,
me!) standing in a shaft of sunlight in an Istanbul mosque.
Then I picked up a book by Mary Austin, published in
1923: *Everyman's Genius.*

How did I know I should buy that book? It was
probably the table of contents: "Chapter I: What is Genius?"; "Chapter III: The Gifts of Experience"; "Chapter
VII: The Creative Wish"; "Chapter X: Genius and Super-
normal Faculties"; "Chapter XIII: Acquiring Genius";
and, finally, "Chapter XV: Genius and the Creative Life."
Very provocative subjects!

So I came home with the old *Geographic* and Mary
Austin. I have been reading and rereading her ever since.
Not only does she demand a lot of her reader, but her
concepts were totally new to me. Perhaps her language is
that of her times, or perhaps it is uniquely her own. I don't
know. I had a hard time with that book. The first thing I
really understood that would be useful to me was her
pointing out that everyone was either "inner-directed" or

"outer-directed." I realized then that, though all my life I had been outer-directed, I wanted to be inner-directed.

I had always believed I must wear the "right" clothes, read the popular books, go to the plays people were talking about—that is, to be like everyone around me. Mary Austin, showing me how foolish that was, helped me get rid of a lot of useless baggage.

Mary Austin was probably the first to impress on me the importance of meditation, but when I read her instructions on how to meditate, I simply couldn't translate them into something I could do. She wrote, "In Meditation . . . the consciousness is first freed in reverie, then cleared gently and held open, so that the desired incursion from the subconsciousness may take place, welling up and separating itself from other material, which must be gently rejected." Luckily for me, Alan Watts had already given me directions that, though vague, seemed achievable.

I didn't let Mary Austin's language discourage me. I raced on, coming soon to a list of "The things that can be affected by autosuggestion." Surely the term "autosuggestion" meant something that one did oneself. I devoured the list:

"The formation of regular habits of work,
"Regularization of the flow of ideas,
"Intensification of emotional response to experience,
"Control of the recalled reaction,
"Transposition of technique gained in one department of artistic activity to another,
"Securing instant and easy command of all you know,
"The fixation of impressions to be re-examined later."

I am not sure I understand even now the meaning of all those processes, but it was wonderful to hear that someone could "secure instant and easy command" of all she/he knew! I tried to master some of them by simply telling myself over and over that I was mastering them and succeeded in a couple—regular habits of work, for one.

Mary Austin's actions were easier to understand than her instructions. I was especially struck by one of her experiences when she was exploring ancient Indian ruins in the Southwest. She wrote that she had stopped to rest in mid-afternoon and "had fallen into a half trance of heat and sleepy light." She said that by degrees she felt her attention "plucked at and drawn to the other side of the shallow arroyo where I was sitting . . . a persistent call to look . . . behind the big boulder." She got up and walked over and found there a beautiful little stone ax, half buried in the sand.

How I envy her this faculty! I haven't been able to develop it but I hope my grandchildren will have that power.

I wonder now why I wasn't more disappointed in *Everyman's Genius*. It promised such miracles and then explained how to perform them in language I couldn't understand. I think it was because at that time I didn't dream that I myself could be capable of such astonishing feats, but I found it inspiring to learn that there were people who could.

I know that if I had ever met Mary Austin, she would have intimidated me. She was so far ahead of me! But I learned from her I no longer needed to have the approval of everyone around me. It now occurs to me that it was because of Mary Austin that, later, when a friend with psychic powers told me I was a healer, I was able to believe that he might be right, and even prove it—on myself— years afterwards. (I'll be telling you about that later.)

Mary Austin must have startled her readers in the 1920s, though many of her theories and experiences are fully accepted today. She would not have been surprised by biofeedback, intuitive understanding (she called it "inknowing") and healing through visualization. She cured herself of cancer through "creative prayer." (Autoprayer was another way she described it.)

I don't think we have entirely caught up with Mary Austin yet, though we are closing in on her. One of my fervent hopes is that the next generation, like Mary Austin, will not be influenced by the color of other people's skin.

I have come upon a note made when I was reading Mary Austin:

I feel as if I had been looking for myself since I was fifty, and that prior to that time I had been wandering with my eyes closed through a dangerous forest. And even now I haven't found myself. I haven't freed myself. I still have unexamined notions (inherited or acquired); I have deep-seated prejudices and fears. I know that if I can free myself, the fears will drop away like wraiths of fog. I'm aware of that. And even if I can't see any progress in freeing myself, I must believe—and hope—that it is happening.

I probably don't need to tell you that I am writing this book because I am finally free.

Have you seen the connection between Mary Austin and enjoying your old age? It is more than peripheral, it is vitally important: you must keep your mind open, listen to new ideas, keep that marvelous childhood attitude of wonderment, half believing, not quite disbelieving.

Mrs. Wheelock was not at all like Mary Austin. I am including her here not because I loved her, though I did, but to show you that a person who had never heard of meditation, who did not have to be told she should be "aware," could have a rich old age. It was Mrs. Wheelock's nature to observe and notice. She knew nothing about nutrition but she was one of the sturdiest, healthiest women I have ever known. Mrs. Wheelock, without thinking about it, lived a good life.

When we rented a house for the summer in Maple Corner, we didn't know that we would find ourselves in a place where life was simple, where everyone was friendly. We didn't know we would meet people whom we would never forget. Mrs. Wheelock was one of them.

Maple Corner was a collection of six houses, the school and the Co-op. (The Co-op consisted of a small building holding the post office and a grocery store, with a gas pump in front.)

It was at the Co-op one evening that I first heard of Mrs. Wheelock. We all were gathered there in the late afternoon waiting for the "stage" to arrive with the mail. (They called it the stage, as though it were drawn by four galloping horses, though it was simply a car driven by one of the farmers.)

I remember that evening someone said, "Did you hear that while Frank was painting a rowboat up at Curtis Pond yesterday, he saw Gertrude Wheelock walking down the hill? He said she was moving right along. Seems she had gotten to thinking that it would be nice to have fish for supper that night. So she walked down. Must be all of three miles from her farm. Frank gave her a boat and she rowed herself out onto the pond and caught herself a nice mess of perch. And then walked back up the hill! She's eighty-two if she's a day!"

Someone else said, "Well, she's a remarkable woman. She makes fine hooked and braided rugs and she can spin a thread from most anything. Her grandmother taught her. Maybe you can remember that a man in Florida wrote to ask her to spin some yarn from the coat of his collie dog—he'd been saving the clippings for years, he said. Gertrude did it. It was in the paper, with a color picture of the man wearing his jacket and the dog standing beside him—looked like brothers!"

"I've never met Mrs. Wheelock," I said, regretfully.

"Oh, you should just drive up there. She likes people to come. She's just about always home."

I didn't think I could just drive up there, but one day I mentioned to a friend that my husband had to have a couple of new shirts before we returned to Princeton. "I suppose I've got to go to town some day soon," I added. ("Town" was the capital of the state of Vermont, Montpelier, but no one ever said they were going to the city. They generally said they had to go "down street." Just as they didn't call Curtis Pond the lake it really was.)

My friend said, "Oh, why don't you take his old shirts to Gertrude Wheelock? She'll be glad to turn the collars on them."

Happy to have an excuse to meet Mrs. Wheelock, I took a couple of Fred's shirts and drove up to Mrs. Wheelock's farm. It sat on a ridge overlooking Worcester Mountain, blue in the distance.

I drove slowly after I left the paved road onto her deeply-rutted lane. I stopped the car in front of the low porch where window boxes spilled over with gaudy petunias. On the other side of the grassy driveway, borders of marigolds and zinnias were framed against an airy curtain of delicate sweet peas.

There was no answer to my knock, so I walked toward the great red barn standing in tall grass a hundred yards away, and then I saw, below the barn, a fine, fenced vegetable garden outlined by shiny disks that danced and rattled in the breeze, keeping away the hungry wildlife. And I saw, coming toward me, Mrs. Wheelock, straight and spare, wearing a weathered wide-brimmed straw hat, a faded blue dress and a dark-blue sweater.

She showed me around her garden which she knew more intimately than most people know their houses. She knew if a crow stole a grain of corn from a newly-planted hill. She knew where the cutworm had burrowed underground when the sun came up. (She dug him right out.) She showed me the flattened grass outside the fence. "The deer played there last night," she said. "The moon was real pretty. I hope you saw it."

We walked up to the house and sat on the porch, rocking. The hillside in front of us mounted to the woods, and more woods met the fields beyond the barn. I heard a wild cry far off in the shadows of the forest. I looked over at Mrs. Wheelock.

"A fox, most likely," she said. "There's lots of animals hereabouts. The woodchucks give me the most trouble. In June they traveled through my flower garden, eating down the sweet peas. I keep a shotgun by the front door, but no sooner I see one and go for the gun, seems he's gone!"

"There's something over in the tall grass by the barn," I said.

"I'll give you the binoculars." She leaned over to pick them up from the window sill.

I found I was focusing on a fat porcupine who was wandering through the long grass. Something else was moving, nearer to us, and I looked at a woodchuck, sitting up like a gopher, staring right back at me.

I told Mrs. Wheelock and she said, comfortably, "Must be the same one I tried to get this morning. I was going to have a real good shot when a truck rattled by on the road." Without changing her tone, she added, "There's a humming bird on the honeysuckle."

Mrs. Wheelock enriched my life. I am indebted to her for some unusual expressions. You must have noticed that the woodchucks "traveled" through the flower garden. Later, she gave me a pleasant picture when she said, "I like spring best; I like traveling through the woods, seeing the signs of things coming up."

Another verb she used in her own way was "punch," giving it the sense of being busy or working. "I've been punching around the garden all morning—haven't finished yet."

If you asked Mrs. Wheelock how she was, she always said, "Very fine, thank you!" and who could dispute that!

Mrs. Wheelock and I became friends. My Vermont journals mention her often. I usually made an entry in my journal after a visit.

Mrs. Wheelock came down from upstairs when I knocked. Her thin grey hair was rolled into a neat braided bun as usual. We sat near the door in two rocking chairs drawn face to face. She doesn't have a phone. "Won't have it," she said. "You can't hear them clear. You hint about it but it don't make any different; you can't hear clear." When I admired the handsome grandfather clock, I noticed it was on standard time. It had been made by her grandfather! she told me when I admired it. "Well, yes, I go by standard time " she said, "but I keep one clock for the other, for the television. I get lots of good channels. I get the White Mountains and New York City and two Montreal stations. " I like to think of Mrs. Wheelock watching television in French!

She told me she didn't like the new "substitutes," like Crisco and margarine. "They're nowhere near as good as lard. And if I don't have butter for my bread, I put bacon fat on it." Today she opened up more than usual. Maybe she is beginning to feel I'm a friend. She said, "People talk about getting fat, but if they did some work, they'd get thin enough. People always looking for pleasure, always a new pleasure, well, they've used them all up now and maybe they'll have to find the pleasure in work."

Late one afternoon my husband and I took Mrs. Wheelock to the Strawberry Festival in the nearby village of Adamant. There people made a great fuss over her, but she received their attentions with a certain coolness that reminded me somehow of Queen Mary, especially when she was greeted by a rather gushy visitor from New York. Mrs. Wheelock looked faintly surprised and said, "Do I know you?"

Clearly she didn't like the fuss being made over her. I remembered how a little earlier I had told her my mother would like to meet her. She had responded almost sharply, "What is it about me that interests her?" She didn't want to be considered a "character."

That evening when we brought her home after the party, I saw her softer side. We stood in front of her low porch, saying good-bye. She seemed in no hurry for us to leave, so I said good-bye again. As I walked back to the car, I turned and saw she was still standing, a little uncertainly, just where I had left her. On an impulse I ran back. When I reached her I gave her a hug and then put my cheek on one side of her leathery face and then the other. "A European kiss!" I said.

As if that had set a seal upon a pleasant evening, she beamed and walked up onto the porch, turning to wave as we drove off. As we went down the lane, I was thinking that it was sad that old ladies like Mrs. Wheelock didn't get kissed very often.

Then we went off for two years in Turkey and while we were gone Mrs. Wheelock had a stroke and had to go into a country nursing home in Worcester. When I heard this, I wrote her once or twice before we got back, and as soon as we were again at Maple Corner, I went to see her.

My journal, September 2, 1966: *I went to see Mrs. Wheelock. She didn't remember me for a minute. She was somewhere else. I could understand that; a nursing home is such a bleak place, and she was not alone in the room. A garrulous old woman took part in our conversation, which wasn't long. It was hard for Mrs. Wheelock to get out the words she wanted, which aggravated her greatly. We talked about her farm and my visits there.*

"Is anyone living there now?" I asked.

"I live there!" she said and I knew that was where she had been when I first came into her room.

Twice she said she felt very bad because she couldn't answer my letters from Turkey.

I think she liked the tiny alabaster vase I'd brought her. She held it in her left hand. Her right didn't "work" at all, she said.

I leaned over and kissed her when I left, awkwardly, on her upper lip. She squeezed her eyes shut and worked her face as she said, "I'm so glad you came! I'm so glad to see you!"

She must have been ninety then.

Mrs. Wheelock died about two years later, but I have never lost her, any more than I've lost the little house in Antrim and that mother squirrel.

There will be one more woman who was important to me, Emily Rockwood, my first cousin. It was she who said, "You're not old until you're ninety, but it's best to be prepared."

I saw Emily only once while we were in Antrim but I wrote to her from Vermont. It wasn't until we made the great leap to California, when she was then in a nursing home in Florida, that I got to know her through her letters, as you will too.

But first I want to introduce you to Bennington, Vermont in the next chapter. There I began meditating seriously.

SUMMING UP: Find Mary Austin's *Everyman's Genius* if you can. I'm sure it will encourage you about our potentials, even if we can't quite acquire the insight and skills of Mary Austin.

As for Gertrude Wheelock, there is plenty to learn from her, even if you don't decide to spread bacon fat on your bread. Mrs. Wheelock hadn't heard about cholesterol, I imagine, but I doubt if she would have worried about it. One of the things I learned from Mrs. Wheelock was not to worry about living alone. I've only recently needed to remember how she happily lived all by herself in that remote farmhouse in northern Vermont.

♋

CHAPTER FOUR

Beginning Meditation— and Meeting Carlos Castaneda

A S YOU KNOW, IN THE SUMMER OF 1973 we left that beloved house in Antrim, left the chipmunks, the mother squirrel, and the quiet woods. We moved to Bennington, Vermont.

We rented half of an old two-story wooden house which, we were told, had once been a button factory. Tall, angular, it had since been divided down the middle. We had an upstairs and a downstairs. The owners lived in the other half and Christie, though I was more than double her age, became a warm friend. (Luckily for me, she later moved to California about the same time we did.)

I needed a friend in Bennington. We had just settled into our pleasant new quarters (no chipmunks around, but friendly squirrels in the backyard) when my husband was seized by a form of arthritis that so crippled him he couldn't even turn over in bed at night to see what time it was.

His illness changed my life and changed me. For the first time I was the chauffeur, I filled out the forms for the income tax. I cashed the checks, and I even made all our household decisions, large as well as small. It wasn't long before I discovered I was a good deal more competent than I had realized; it gave me a heady feeling of self-confidence.

My workroom was not ideal. When we moved in, Fred had expected to do a lot of writing so we decided he should take the dining room for his workplace, so he soon moved in his files and spread his papers out on the big table. When it turned out he was too ill to manage the stairs, I didn't like to make his illness appear permanent by taking over his space.

I settled into a small room at the top of the stairs, opposite the bathroom. The ceiling slanted on one side but I was able to tuck a cot under its protection. I set up my typewriter near the window which looked down on the tree-lined street. My files were near the door. It was cozy—but not private.

At first I found it difficult to meditate in this little room. I could hear Fred moving around, a plane going overhead, a car coming up the street. Then somewhere I picked up the idea that it helped to meditate on an object. I chose a fat green candle in a glass cup supported by glass vines twining up from a flat base. To my surprise, the candle shut out the world.

I recorded the experience regularly in my journal.

It's interesting that every day the candle experience is different. Yesterday the flame never appeared above the rim of the crater of wax. Today it stood strong and bright above the candle, burning brilliantly, but as I watched, it gradually changed, turning into a round flower with an open center, like a pinwheel or a little pansy. It danced and twinkled but grew gradually more fragile, and finally disappeared below the rim of the wax.

I began to get absorbed in meditation. I often used the candle, as I found it always held my attention without any effort on my part.

In Antrim I had never gotten beyond the fifteen-minute meditation and I had made a note in my journal:

I'm still not ready to act, not ready to believe in the inherent power in an individual, in myself. I think I believe but I'm not willing to go off the high board. I am afraid.

I didn't believe that meditation would actually help me and I still hadn't accepted Mary Austin's revelations.

But in Bennington, I was beginning to spend more than fifteen minutes meditating and I was beginning to feel that meditation was making a difference. Now, after all these years of working on it, I have learned that you don't have to be very good at it. You don't have to spend a lot of time on it. But if you keep at it, meditating regularly every day, the miraculous thing is that you will recognize there has been a change. You may be surprised by someone saying, unexpectedly, "Have you noticed that you are not so tense these days? You're much more relaxed. What's going on?"

If you think your friend will laugh if you answer, "I've been meditating," then just smile and say, "I really hadn't noticed, but you may be right."

I might warn you that you will be very lucky if you come across someone who understands what you are trying to do. I wrote in my journal a few years after I began meditating:

I don't know a single person, I mean I haven't a single friend, not even an acquaintance, who empties her/his mind. Being a mind-emptier is almost as lonely an addiction as being a writer.

I have to confess I am a wretched meditator. I read with awe of people who meditate for an hour, two hours, or even a whole day. I can never manage more than twenty or thirty minutes and even then I peek at the clock a couple of times before the timer goes off. But I can testify that even such a poor performer is changed. I myself had a friend remark on it. (My husband!)

Meditation can be very simple. I'll go over it. You must first find a quiet place at a time of day when you know you won't be interrupted for at least fifteen minutes. When you have located this place, sit down in a straight chair with your feet squarely on the floor, back straight, head tilted just slightly forward. When you are comfortable in this position, lay your right hand in your left hand and touch your thumbs together. Then relax. Meditation is almost pure relaxation.

Now try to empty your mind of thoughts. The thoughts will return, they will surge through, but ignore them. Let them go by. The easiest way for me is to ignore my thoughts and to count my breaths as they come in and out. I count up to ten and then begin again, going by tens up to one hundred. Sometimes I find it helpful to visualize the numbers as I count them. If my thoughts grab me for a moment, I go back and begin again. Instead of breath-counting, some people use a "mantra," which can be any simple word or phrase, repeated over and over, silently. I often use the Tibetan chant *Om Mani Padme Hum.* (This is generally translated as "Hail to the Jewel in the Lotus.")

Occasionally I simply look at the inner landscape I see when my eyes are closed. I may see an empty plain with dirt roads crossing it to distant mountains; sometimes I am granted a vision of a deep blue wave boiling up from a void. And sometimes I see nothing at all.

If you become serious about meditation, there are a good many experts who can steer you better than I, and take you further. I'll list some of them in the back of this book.

I'll say once again, that if you keep on trying to meditate regularly, you will find the rewards of even amateurish meditation stunning.

I am now thinking of my young friends, Sue, Pam, Cynthia and Christie. I am wondering if you have begun to feel that you could never find a quiet fifteen minutes in your present life.

It is a hard fact that if you want to make the most of your old age, you probably will have to change, and change doesn't come easily or painlessly. You will need to apply self-discipline. If you haven't yet acquired it, now is the time to develop it, at least enough to hold to fifteen minutes of quiet every day.

You may think that it's too late for you to try to change yourself, that your habits are too deeply rooted, that you are too old to experiment with odd and difficult exercises, but I must tell you that I don't think anyone is too old to change, just as I think anyone can learn a new skill at any age.

A Turkish doctor, my friend Jahit Bey, told me years ago, "The brain is like a muscle. It will atrophy if you don't use it, but if you keep on using it, it will get stronger."

You may remember that I had my sixty-third birthday while I was living in that little house in the woods. I can now say with confidence that sixty isn't too old to start out on this new road.

I can see from this distance that what I did was in a way to remake myself, and that is probably what you may have to do, too. *The foundation on which you will build this new self is meditation. It is the single most important element in making yourself over.*

To turn to a lighter subject, I once did an experiment that seemed like magic. I didn't repeat it because, I think,

I was afraid it wouldn't come again to such a splendid finale a second time.

I had bought a book by Laura Archera Huxley, *You Are Not The Target*. I still use the catchy title as a touchstone when I am made uncomfortable by some caustic remark, for Laura Huxley suggested one should always look further, look below the surface for the cause of the remark. She felt the bitterness was often aimed at the nearest person, though actually reflecting a hurt or insult someone else had inflicted upon the speaker.

In addition to this useful reminder, the book contained an interesting exercise that I tried at once.

In my journal I gave the exercise a title: BEAUTIFUL FOR THE FIRST TIME:

I have been doing Laura Huxley's exercise. The main feature is holding your arms above your head. She says it's no good doing it for less than ten minutes, but my arms ached right away when I did it and I did it for only three minutes. Even so, the exercise worked!

I did it standing in front of a small mirror but, as I was told to do, I kept my eyes shut. At first keeping my eyes shut made me feel dizzy, perhaps because I remembered hearing that old people lose their balance if they stand or walk with their eyes shut. (I am seventy now.) But I told myself this doesn't have to be true and, though I felt a little giddy, I didn't sway.

Then the first time experience. When I opened my eyes and looked in the mirror, I thought incredulously, "Why, I'm beautiful!" The mirror showed my hair was soft and fluffy around my face, my position was graceful, below my shoulders my body tapered to a narrow waist.

I gave my instinctive denial: "It's because I'm not wearing my glasses. I can't see my wrinkles and jowls."

But even before I had wrinkles and jowls, I never thought I was pretty, not even especially nice-looking and certainly not beautiful.

When I think about this now, it somehow reminds me of a "portrait" an artist-friend did of me, showing the colors he saw around me. It doesn't look like me but it says nice things about me, and perhaps what I saw in the mirror was the same sort of vision, perhaps not me but what I might be. Anyway, both the exercise and the "portrait" gave me a real lift. I don't pretend to understand how Laura Huxley's exercise made me, for a moment, beautiful, but I usually smile when I remember it.

It was about then I began reading about a true magician, at least that is the way I see Carlos Castaneda. He opened my eyes to possibilities even wilder and stranger than those of Mary Austin. Only now am I beginning to grasp the underlying truths that he was demonstrating.

Carlos Castaneda first caught my attention in December, 1972, when Steven Roberts had a piece about him in *The New York Times* in which he said, "Don Juan's central premise is that the world as we know it is only one version of 'reality,' a set of 'agreements' and 'descriptions' that are embedded in the culture and 'pounded into our heads since we have been children.'" And then quoting Castaneda himself, "[Don Juan] was concerned with giving me another description of the world, another way of seeing another reality."

This idea was placed almost within my reach later in the article.

"He [Castaneda] feels one can 'see' the separate reality through concentration and through a variety of exercises that disrupt the habit of daily life and freshen the senses."

I can't explain why these ideas took such hold of me but I began to read Castaneda's books as they came out. I hovered over them dizzily, mesmerized.

An anecdote I read in a *Harper's* article about Castaneda (February, 1973) by Gweneth Craven has amused me ever since.

"Carlos Castaneda is driving his tan Volkswagen bus along a boulevard that takes us through the greater Los Angeles area and oceanward."

"I was having car trouble," he says, "Don Juan told me to talk to my car and make it an extension of myself. I said, 'Come on, don Juan, it's just a machine! That would be insane.' He said, 'The car operates from power and under power. It is the power you must talk to.' I did and my car is now a warrior's car. It's just a stupid Volkswagen like anybody else's, but if I run out of gas, it's in front of a gas station.' He beams. 'It's a matter of talking to power.'"

Some years later I came upon a copy of Mary Austin's autobiography, *Earth Horizon,* and there was Mary Austin describing Tony Luhan, a Taos Pueblo Indian, who was driving her through the mountains of New Mexico. She said, "Tony is an exceptionally good driver . . . making the car an extension of his personality. *Tony puts the car on.*" (My emphasis.)

It's the same thing really, isn't it? I think the reason I enjoy hearing such stories is that it is so liberating to discover someone has developed to the extent that he / she can make an inanimate object an ally.

I was drawn to Castaneda for another reason: He explained quite clearly how he "dreamed" his books. I thought this was a wonderful idea. He suggested that one begins by thinking of an object before going to sleep and then looking for it in a dream. I tried this from October 1973 to August 1975, off and on. The object I always tried to see was my hands, and I did see them three times, but I could also see that I wasn't going to dream my books, so I gave up.

But Castaneda liberated me in his own peculiar way, as I noted in my journal in 1975. My son, Douglas, had come with his wife to visit us in Bennington and later I made this note in my journal:

*When Doug and Karen and I were discussing Castaneda—
it must have been at least two years ago—Karen said, "But if
you really believed him, believed it was not a put-on, then you'd
have to change your life."*

*I am wondering now if, in some subtle way, my life hasn't
changed because of Castaneda, though I couldn't say exactly in
what way.*

This isn't as abrupt a change as you may think; I am
going to take you back to Antrim for a minute. While we
were there an event took place that probably changed my
life as much as Mary Austin and Carlos Castaneda. We
had flown to California to have a visit with our trans-
planted younger son, John, and his family. On the way
back at the San Francisco airport, I picked up something to
read on the flight back. I didn't know I was making a
momentous decision when I chose an oversized paper-
back, *The Well Body Book,* by Mike Samuels, M.D. and Hal
Bennett.

I didn't know exactly why I chose it, for I hadn't yet
begun to realize that my body was an important part of me
that needed to be more than casually looked after.

I probably riffled through it on the plane but I must
have decided it was not a book for amusement or distrac-
tion. In fact, it is difficult for me now to remember how I
felt about *The Well Body Book* when I first dipped into it. I
suspect I felt just as some of you who are reading this
would feel if I handed you a copy. You'd say, "Too
fantastic! I could never do that! How could anyone?"

I do remember that the explicit illustrations of body
parts surprised me, though I suppose they wouldn't surprise anyone today, even me.

At any rate, I put it among my books as if it were an
ordinary book, though it was actually a time bomb ticking
quietly away until I was ready for it. That time was not far
off. In Bennington it wasn't long before I found I needed

help and something made me turn at last to *The Well Body Book*. There I found what I was looking for and I began a routine that I have kept up ever since. Although most of the exercises were prosaic enough, there was one even more startling than Laura Huxley's.

In the next chapter I'll tell you about the event that drove me to *The Well Body Book* for help. Fred's terrible illness was swallowing me up too—not only taking my time but my energy and my natural optimism. *The Well Body Book* has simple exercises for deep relaxation and I began then a routine I still keep up. I do a relaxation every day and often twice.

SUMMING UP: It is vital that you follow the advice for meditation that you have just been given. It will develop the self-discipline you must acquire. If you would like to read about a couple of people who learned to meditate under the most rigid conditions, get hold of the book, by Janwillem van de Wetering and Jane Hamilton-Merritt.

≤

CHAPTER FIVE

Learning to Relax: Its Unexpected Rewards

M Y LIFE IN BENNINGTON had become a series of stark contrasts. Sometimes I felt I was growing stronger and more self-confident, but more often I felt the weight of Fred's painful illness. After an unsuccessful stay in the Bennington Hospital, I had driven him over to Hanover, New Hampshire, to the Dartmouth teaching hospital for further examination. Feeling unreal, I endured several long nights and dreary days, waiting for the doctors to decide his fate. In the end we were given no decision, and no diagnosis, and we went back to Bennington again, feeling hopeless.

It was during these unhappy days that our son, Doug, and his wife came for the weekend. I was overjoyed at the prospect. I prepared an elaborate dinner, drove the fifty miles to the Amtrak station in New York State and brought them back to Bennington. That night we sat up late talking.

The next morning Fred was (mercifully) sleeping late and the guest room was quiet. (I was sleeping as usual on my cot in my work room). I knew I had to get up to start breakfast and plan lunch, but I was dead tired. I forced myself to get out of bed, dressed and started down the stairs. Suddenly a wave of hopelessness, fatigue and self-pity flooded over me and I simply didn't look for the next step. I moved out into empty space.

The crash woke the sleepers. I hadn't broken any bones, and was only badly bruised. I was helped to my cot and later someone brought me breakfast. I suppose my ego was purring.

At any rate, on the drive back alone from the Amtrak station on Sunday night, I realized that I had to get hold of myself somehow. The next time I felt so desperate, I might have a serious accident. It was then that I looked for *The Well Body Book* and began to try its suggestions for handling tension and emotional problems. I couldn't have found a better friend.

Soft bound, it is a fat book by Mike Samuels, M.D., and Hal Bennett. I am looking at it now, its yellow cover still bright. I flip through the pages. I find I am stopping to read "Disease as a Positive Force." Such an interesting concept! Now I have skipped to the end to read "How I came to write this book," and I think Mike's reason for writing it was still valid. He wrote it, he said, because as a doctor, he found people knew very little about their bodies. (I was a prime example.) The book not only corrects this, but gives suggestions that make it easier for us to take care of them.

It was his relaxation exercises that I knew I needed. I tried most of them and soon put several on tape. I even taped their list of the ways to use relaxation: "To relax your whole body when you feel fatigue, to relax your mind and body when you feel emotional conflict, anxiety, grief from loss or emotional upset of any kind. Relax your body in order to increase circulation when you feel the first symptoms of an illness," etc. (I've listened to that tape so often, I just about wrote the quote by heart.)

Now, twenty years later, I still listen to the relaxation tapes every day. I know by now that they are essential to my well-being.

When I began these exercises, it was rather like beginning meditation; I didn't really believe they would be effective, but three things happened that proved to me their value and effectiveness.

The Well Body Book offered a short exercise they called "centering." They claimed that a quick way to calm and relax yourself was to concentrate on your center, just below your navel. If you sent your thoughts, your distress, your anxiety to your center, along with your breath and the attention of your whole body, "You'll be quite surprised by the benefits," they said.

Though I didn't put this on tape, something made me remember it some weeks later when I needed it.

We had been asked to lunch by an old friend who lived a long drive from us, in northern Vermont (Bennington is on the southern border of Massachusetts, almost in Massachusetts). My husband, of course, couldn't undertake the day-long excursion, but he urged me to go. However, he first had me have the car checked over at the local garage. We had full confidence in our Saab, but Fred was nervous about my making the long journey alone.

It was a beautiful fall day, the trees ablaze with gaudy colors. I had a delightful visit. I started back early, feeling very cheerful, but as I was driving through a stretch of lonely woods, the dashboard in front of me lit up with red lights. Every possible danger signal blazed. I panicked. I lost my head. I thought the car was going to catch on fire!

Should I jump out? No house in sight, no other cars on this country road. My heart beat wildly. I turned off the engine, the alarms subsided but what to do?

What made me think of *The Well Body Book* and its centering exercise? Even stranger was that I could remember its instructions. I followed them exactly and in the few minutes it took, my mind returned to normal. I felt sure that nothing really terrifying was about to happen.

I turned on the engine. Nothing exploded, though the red lights flared their warning again. I warily put the car in gear and moved slowly forward. I hoped I would come upon a gas station or a house or a person before long.

I suppose it wasn't a mile before I came to a village and gas station, though at the time it seemed hours. I got some gas, turned the engine on and demonstrated my problem. A man there who had a Saab didn't know what the trouble was but he thought if I drove back to Bennington slowly and carefully, that I would make it all right. I made it.

The alarm system never went on again, but I have done that centering on other stressful occasions, like waiting in a doctor's office or flying in bad weather in a thunder storm. I feel better for knowing that I can use it, and it always works!

Almost by accident, I found that relaxing actually can stop pain. I had unexpectedly had a severe gripping pain which my doctor told me was probably in my colon, so I had to have one of those very uncomfortable examinations. The specialist found no signs of anything serious. Later my doctor told me that it was simply a spasm and that no one knew what caused it or how to cure it.

Then in my journal: *May 22, 1976: An extraordinary thing! Night before last about 2 AM I had that same terrifying colon pain. There is something in the quality of the pain, as if it were an open wound, that panics me.*

But I remembered my doctor had said it was actually a spasm. Thinking a spasm might be helped by relaxing, I tried The Well Body Book's *relaxation exercise, though my heart was pounding with anxiety and I was filled with elemental pain.*

Gradually, by forcing my mind to concentrate on the exercise and not on the pain, the pain began to recede. Before I had gotten through the exercise twice, it was gone and I fell asleep! What wonderful hope this gives me!

I was beginning to find I had more control over my body than I ever had dreamed. I wrote my son, Doug, about one of my early successes: *By accident I cut the inside of my mouth close to a tooth; it was very painful. I woke in the middle of the night because it was throbbing regularly and really hurt.*

I tried emptying my mind and I must have slowed my pulse because almost right away the throbbing slowed down and I noticed that the pain seemed to be far away, as if it were on the southern horizon and my mind in an open empty plain on the northern horizon. The pain didn't bother me any more and I fell asleep.

A couple of hours later I went through the whole performance again and then slept the rest of the night. The throbbing was gone when I woke.

I find it exciting to think that perhaps I'll be able to exercise some control over pain and emotion in this way.

It was about then that both our sons, Doug and John, had settled in California and began coaxing us to join them out there. We were able to do this in 1977 because the incredible happened. A New York specialist in rheumatoid arthritis, a friend of our son, Doug, examined Fred and found he had a form of arthritis for which there was a quick remedy, so he had promptly recovered.

It was just a couple of months before we were to leave that I woke up one morning with ugly eruptions on my thigh. Over the phone the doctor diagnosed shingles and recommended aspirin. Aspirin! Shingles are very painful. I was desperate.

My journal: *The pain the first week of the shingles was stunning. It was concentrated in my right thigh but seemed to flood through my whole body, like flames burning in the hollows of my body. I have never felt anything just like it.*

At first I found that as it surged up, I tightened my whole body to withstand it. I clenched my teeth and stiffened my muscles. I held myself tense until the wave of pain subsided for a few moments.

Then it occurred to me that I was doing just the wrong thing. When the pain hit me again, I tried to relax my body. I discovered that pain disappeared!

The nights were particularly difficult—so long and so painful—but when I could make myself do a relaxation exercise, I would fall asleep and often slept for half an hour. This partial control of the pain and the soothing effect of Vitamin E cream on those virulent spots helped enormously.

Am I making all this sound easy? Have I made you feel that I learned all this very quickly? On the contrary, it has taken years, but I can tell you now that, since I have the usual troubles of old age, I find it a relief to be able to subdue arthritis pains or any other grumbles my body may produce. Since I am a slow learner, as I have told you before, it is possible if you try relaxing when you have a simple pain you will succeed quite quickly.

There's one more recommendation in *The Well Body Book* that I want to tell you about. I've been tiptoeing around it in my mind: *Shall I tell them? They'll think I'm crazy. I can't tell them. But I must.*

The Well Body Book suggests that we find an Imaginary Doctor. As they describe her/him, it really does sound crazy. And one of my difficulties is that I have always had trouble relating to doctors. They seem to center their attention not on me, but on whatever is troubling me, as if it had more reality than I did.

I had begun to trust *The Well Body Book,* but I hesitated. I decided to ask "Mary" what she thought about the Imaginary Doctor. Mary was a silent voice I heard in the middle of the night or at dawn, when I couldn't sleep and was puzzling about the book I was trying to write. Mary had become very real to me and I was wondering what she looked like. I recorded her answer in my journal.

March 29, 1976, 6 AM:

I: "How about it, Mary? Couldn't I try to visualize you, see you as an actual person?"

Mary: "I don't know why. I'm not an actual person. I'm only another aspect of you. I think visualizing me would be on a par with picturing God as an old man with a long white beard and a benign expression!"

I: "Well, what about that Imaginary Doctor? Can you act in that role?"

Mary: "'Act in that role' is just what it would be: an act. But The Well Body Book *people aren't calling for play acting; they are using real magic. The doctor, in order to be powerful, to be able to touch a sore spot and heal it, has to be alive and breathing. Otherwise the magic would not work."*

I think it was that word *magic* that made me decide to try the "Imaginary Doctor" exercise.

SUMMING UP: The simple exercises described in this chapter can spare you the panic caused by a frightening experience, and also remove, at least temporarily, an unpleasant pain. And while such mysterious entities as "Mary" and the imaginary doctor you will hear about in the next chapter are not an essential part of learning how to manage your old age, I have found them friendly companions who have made this journey easier.

CHAPTER SIX

♀

My Imaginary Doctor

THE YEAR 1976 WAS VERY DIFFICULT since Fred's illness had not been given a diagnosis. He was up and down, but mostly down. We finally decided it would be easier for him if we were in a house of only one story, so we had bought one.

The new house was built on the side of a hill with the garage in the basement which was above ground. The basement also had a little room whose window looked across a smooth lawn to a big willow tree where the little girls of the neighborhood often played house with their dolls. I seized it for my workroom.

The workroom was okay. I couldn't hear the telephone or the doorbell from it, though I could hear Fred walking over my head.

Perhaps if my life had been as easy and cheerful as it had been in Antrim, I might not have felt such a strong urge to get help from my own inner resources. I had already found "Mary, " who had become as real to me as the people I was seeing on the street in Bennington. (Mary wasn't easy on me, but when I read over my records of her remarks about the book I was writing, I can see she was right on the mark, painful though I had found them at the time.)

I was using the exercises in *The Well Body Book* but still I hadn't summoned up the courage to try their Imaginary Doctor exercise, when I remembered a remark Georgia O'Keefe had made about a fellow artist who hadn't quite made it: "She lacked nerve. You have to have nerve!" That did it. I picked up *The Well Body Book* and turned to page 6, "Create your imaginary doctor." So, tucked away in my new work room like one of those chipmunks in winter quarters in Antrim, I began a new adventure.

The Well Body Book was very explicit. Imagine a comfortable house, open the door and go into it. You will find your own room in it with no trouble. When you are in your room and the door is closed, the doctor will come.

When I began, I didn't know what to expect—or rather, *whom* to expect. I was nervous, so I did a relaxation exercise that helped. Then I imagined an old house in northern Vermont. It was a two-story, white clapboard house, and I walked up a dirt road and found it. It faced a little woods. Zinnias and pansies had been planted by the front door by someone, but no one was around. There was a knocker on the door, but I didn't knock. I opened the door and walked in. I didn't hear anyone, though the house didn't seem vacant. I thought everyone must have gone out for a while.

In front of me was a broad, carpeted staircase which mounted to a landing and there branched left and right. I went slowly up, and took the left stairway which brought me to a long corridor with doors along the left side. I walked its full length and at the last door I took a key out of my pocket and opened the door. It was as if I had done it all before.

I found myself in a small room, facing a window that looked out on an old maple tree. A squirrel was racing along an upper branch. There were two chairs in the room. I tried to remember my instructions. I was to open the door that was across from the chairs, but I hadn't been told just how to do it. The door would slide upwards from the floor. I sat down in a chair facing it and then simply willed it to open. I felt foolish as well as nervous. My journal picks it up here:

May 9, 1976: I'm not really expecting to meet anyone here in this little room, but suddenly I have the impression that a man's dark eyes are laughing—not at me, but at the situation.

Then the door lifts slowly. I see strong, square feet, bare, wearing leather sandals and before I am ready he is there, standing in front of me.

His face is roundish, not quite brown, but not white either— a good living color, not a dead color like white. His hair is black and curly, a bit disheveled. He is looking at me, cheerfully. His mouth is big, his lips full. He is wearing jeans with a broad leather belt which has a silver, turquoise-studded buckle. He is not particularly tall, rather stocky, heavy rather than slight. His hands, made hard and muscular through work, have the long, delicate fingers of an artist or a surgeon.

A laugh is lingering on his lips. I knew he had been amused to be waiting behind the door, waiting for me to open it and look at him.

He tells me his name is Jaime (High-mee) and he is a Mexican Indian. He looks at me, almost as if asking permission, and sits down in the other chair.

I feel shy. I am conscious that I am seventy years old and he's a young man. He knows immediately what I am thinking.

"I will never laugh at you!" he says. He means he would never feel cause to, not that he would hide it.

"We will shake hands," he says, and gets up and comes

*forward, taking my hand in both of his. His hands are warm and
strong.*

"Can you help me?" I ask.

"I think so," he answers. "I hope so. I will try."

"We will talk again," I say. *I feel the whole situation is too
strange for me to take in.*

"All right," *he says and starts for the open space left by that
special door. Then he turns and comes back.* "We will shake
hands again," *and again he takes my hand between both of his.
He turns to walk toward the door, his strong back toward me and
the door descends and he is gone.*

Since that first conversation, I have talked to Jaime
about thirty times (so far). I'm still consulting him. I called
for him most often that year when I was under such stress
in Vermont. He became more and more helpful. At first I
had questions about him which I asked him soon after I
met him. For instance:

May 11, 1976.

"I really don't know why you do this, Jaime."

Jaime: "I like to help people. I really like to. You like to help
people, too. Maybe you'll do this some day too."

I (flabbergasted): "Are you a real person, Jaime? Do you
exist somewhere?"

Jaime: "Yes, in a way. But not as you see me exactly. The
way you see me is the way I want to be. So, you see, we react on
each other. We each give to the other."

I: "But your 'doctor' role? How does that work?"

Jaime: "I can see you clearer than you can see yourself, that's
all. I can see what you need. And I'm closer to the old resources
than you are. Of course it would be nice if you could see clearly
for yourself, and maybe you will be able to some day."

I: "Thank you, Jaime." (I give him my hand.) "I'll see you
soon. Maybe tomorrow. Anyway, today has been a good day;
I've been surprised by my energy."

Reading that again, I wonder if I ever will be able to see myself clearly. But I realize that I have learned a good deal from Jaime.

To show you how slow I was to learn how to take care of myself, I will give you another conversation with Jaime when I was being troubled by a persistent headache:

July 28, 1976

I: "Well, Jaime?" (He is looking at me, gently but reproachfully.)

Jaime: "We should have talked before this. You haven't wanted to, have you?"

I: "I was afraid of what you'd tell me I would have to do. I thought you'd tell me I must not try to do all the things I want to do."

Jaime: "You knew that without my telling you. I guess the headache tells you."

I: "You think that the headache is my friend, I guess. But I think it is an enemy, hurting me, stopping me. Mornings I can't even make plans for the afternoon without adding, 'If the headache doesn't come on.'"

Jaime: "When it's so serious, we have to be serious about it, don't we?"

I: "What can we do?"

And there I stop. It's as if the headache had hung a heavy curtain between Jaime and me. I can't see him. I can't hear him. Jaime, are you there? I hear nothing. I shut my eyes and listen. I still can't hear him. There's something between us. Is it the headache or is it resistance on my part, still afraid of what he'll say? I'm going to lie on the cot on the sun deck. Perhaps there I'll be able to hear him

Later, in my journal:

I didn't get Jaime to speak to me but I began to see I need a positive attitude. My whole outlook is negative. "If this headache hangs on, I won't be able to—we won't be able to—have friends for the weekend, go to the Conservation meeting in Stratton, go to California."

So I got out The Well Body Book *and read it for half an hour. And I found I must work for a better attitude. I should do the energy exercises regularly and, most important, I must pace myself—not give up what I most enjoy doing (writing) but go slower at everything, do less of everything; less of having people here, less of going out, less cooking of fancy food (I was planning a quiche for supper) etc. I will try.*

I think I'll give you one of the last conversations I had with Jaime before we left for California, though after we settled in California I had at least one very unusual visit with Jaime, that I will tell you about in its proper place. But this Vermont conversation applies particularly to what we are talking about in this book.

July 17, 1976: I had been talking with Jaime and as usual he was telling me not to do so much, to hold myself back. And I said, "I was even thinking, Jaime, that my wings have been clipped all my life, and I have wondered what I would have done if I had had full use of them. I decided, though, that I wouldn't have done as much as I dream I would have, because actually I haven't much talent."

Then Jaime said: "Talent! Everyone has talent if they relax and let it out. Telling yourself you haven't much talent is like telling yourself not to eat too much because you have a small stomach. Your stomach can stretch and so can your abilities. Tap your inner resources and you can do anything!"

I said, "Isn't it too late at my age?"

Jaime: "'At your age!' I never thought to hear you say that. You're much more tired than I realized. Tell me, what is age? Nothing! You know that age has no reality except physically. You should forget your age."

I remembered my Turkish friend, Dr. Jahit Bey, saying the same thing, "I never thought to hear you say, 'at my age'!" That was in 1964. I wondered if I would ever learn that lesson.

I never ceased being astonished by Dr. Jaime, who was not at all what I had expected when I went through *The Well Body Book* exercise to meet him. I had thought that my friendly Turkish doctor might appear, or Mary Austin or even Carlos Castaneda, but I had not expected a young Mexican-Indian named Jaime.

Perhaps this is where I should confess that I have just discovered (in 1994) that I mis-remembered my instructions. I should have told the door to open from the top down. But, as you know, this made no difference; it worked anyway.

I have told some of my good friends about this experience. Two or three surprised me by looking for their own Imaginary Doctors. *The Well Body Book* says your doctor may turn out to be a person, an animal or a light beam; It could be an old woman, a dog, someone from outer space or a disembodied voice. One of my friends discovered hers was a Japanese woman, another that hers was a healer dressed all in white, and the third heard the healer's disembodied voice when she found herself sitting on a sandy desert in a circle of light.

I don't know whether my friends have kept in contact with their "doctors," but I know that I resist calling Jaime much as I resist meditation. I think one reason I don't go to that quiet old house in Vermont very often is because I am a coward. Jaime so often tells me something I don't want to hear. For instance: *Me: "Do you think I should see a doctor?" Jaime: "Yes, you had better make an appointment this morning!"*

I didn't talk to Dr. Jaime for four years after those troubled talks in 1976 and I've talked to him only a few times since. Altogether I have recorded twenty-eight conversations between mid-1976 and 1993.

Perhaps one of the reasons is that I am not only a slow learner, but I am a slow believer! In Bennington I believed in Dr. Jaime, and yet, at another level, his existence

seemed incredible to me. Still, over the years I have discovered that a lot of ideas I had thought unbelievable are
perfectly possible, and I now take Dr. Jaime as seriously as
he deserves. There is one statement in *The Well Body Book*
that I still find incredible. It's on page 8: "The imaginary
doctors might have an objective reality of their own;
several people report having met their imaginary doctors
in real life after creating them in the exercise."

SUMMING UP: You may be inclined to dismiss the very
idea of an imaginary doctor but I suggest that you don't
quite forget it, for the day may come when you are in
desperate need of advice that you don't feel you can bring
up with your competent, but very orthodox, internist.

♋

CHAPTER SEVEN

Ouspensky Introduces Gurdjieff; Angels Appear

N OW IT IS TIME TO TELL YOU ABOUT a strange and mysterious man, a mystic, a philosopher, a teacher. Of Greek, Russian and Turkish ancestry, brought up in southern Russia before the Revolution of 1917, he traveled through the Far East studying with dervish and other esoteric sects, and finally came to the West, establishing a school in France to teach what he had learned. Later he lectured in New York. Peter Brook made a beautiful film of his early life, based on Gurdjieff's book, *Meetings with Remarkable Men*. His full name was George Ivanovitch Gurdjieff. Born in 1872, he died in Paris in 1949. Even today groups of people meet to study his ideas.

I first heard of Gurdjieff in Adam Smith's book, *The Powers of the Mind*. Adam Smith made him sound interesting, but I hadn't been able to find any books by Gurdjieff, which was just as well, as they might have put me off him forever. His books are written in a difficult, convoluted language, some of which he invented himself.

However, one wet April evening in Bennington, Christie, our young landlady, took us to have dinner with a lawyer, also young, who lived in a converted railroad station in Arlington. His dining room was long and shadowy, lit by candles on the refectory table. It was the right atmosphere for good talk, which we had. Later, when I wanted to look at the books which lined the walls almost to the high ceiling, our host switched on some lights.

I saw a fat blue-and-white paperback, *In Search of the Miraculous*, by P.D. Ouspensky. I loved the title. I didn't know I was making an important decision when I asked if I could borrow it. I took it home, elated. Such a nice fat book would keep me busy for quite a while. I didn't know it would absorb me the rest of my life.

Ouspensky had spent years with Gurdjieff and although I couldn't understand all his explanations of Gurdjieff's ideas, I was fascinated by the adventures of this dedicated group during the perilous days of the Revolution in Russia. I read the book so slowly that I finally called to apologize for keeping it so long, but John said, laughing, "Oh, keep it! I've gone as far as I can with Gurdjieff!"

I kept it. I still have it. As I raise my eyes from my typewriter I see it up there on my bookshelf, among a whole clutch of books by and about Gurdjieff.

I have stopped here. It's so difficult to explain to you the effect Gurdjieff had on me. Before I tackle that, however, I'll digress for a moment to repeat to you something that Peter Brook, who made that film about Gurdjieff, said in an interview, for it is something we might think about.

Peter Brook, discussing Gurdjieff, also digressed. He said that when he traveled in the London Underground he looked at the faces of the older people and wondered why they had "declined." Later, traveling in Africa and Afghanistan, he visited villages where the opposite was true.

"Their faces got more and more beautiful, and their inner strength amply compensates for anything declining in their outer strength. At the end of their lives—like trees—they are at their strongest and most beautiful." I wondered then why that was. Is it that our amusements, our distractions, our indulgences, wear away the beauty that we could otherwise have in our old age? This renewed my determination not to "decline" as I grew older.

To get back to Ouspensky's book, *In Search of the Miraculous,* I first read it as if I were reading a novel, but it wasn't long before I came upon some extraordinary ideas, essentially simple ideas, that I could agree with. Gurdjieff was convinced that people in general were asleep, (yes, you and me, too), that we aren't aware of what we are doing or why we are doing it. Habit, convention, inertia? Probably all three. Being asleep is easier than being awake, but I knew as I read this that I wanted to be awake. I didn't want to live the rest of my life in a dream; I knew too many people who were doing just that. (Gurdjieff didn't know he was echoing Mary Austin, or was she echoing him?)

I began to take seriously the exercise Gurdjieff recommended for waking up. "Self-Remembering," he called it. It is a little different from the current "Mindfulness," which as I understand it, is simply noticing everything. I came across a definition of self-remembering that I think is clear: "Self-remembering is subtly different from self-observation; it means being aware of yourself and your surroundings, your mind occupied with your situation, not with extraneous matters." (This was in Thomas de Hartmann's excellent book about his life with Gurdjieff.)

Ouspensky, in *In Search of the Miraculous,* has such a clear description of how it is to self-remember that I am quoting it to you in full. It must have been about 1915 when Ouspensky wrote that he was walking in St. Petersburg, trying to remember himself.

"... In spite of all my efforts, I was unable to keep my attention on self-remembering. The noise, movement, everything distracted me. Every minute I lost the thread of attention, found it again, and then lost it again. ... [I] firmly decided to keep my attention on the fact that I *would remember myself* at least for some time. . . I reached the Nadejdinskaya without losing the thread of attention, except perhaps for short moments. ... I reached the Nevsky still remembering myself, and was already beginning to experience the strange emotional state of inner peace and confidence which comes after great efforts of this kind. Just around the corner on the Nevsky was a shop where they made my cigarettes. Still remembering myself, I thought I would call there and order some cigarettes.

"Two hours later I *woke up* in the *Tavricheskaya*, that is, far away. I was going by *Izvostchik* to the printers. The sensation of awakening was extraordinarily vivid. I can almost say I *came to*. I remembered everything at once. How I had been walking along the Nadejdinskaya, remembering myself, how I had thought about cigarettes and how at this thought I seemed all at once to fall and disappear into a deep sleep."

Ouspensky then described all the things he had done in those two hours and then, as he was driving to the printers, he began to feel a strange uneasiness, "... as though I had forgotten something. *And suddenly I remembered that I had forgotten to remember myself.*"

Self-remembering is a tantalizing exercise. We feel it must be easy to be aware of our surroundings and at the same time notice how we are feeling, both physically and emotionally. In fact, it seems as if we were always doing just that. Not so! You will find, very quickly, if you are "awake," that even a car coming down the street will set you off on a different track. It is rather like the challenge of meditating, though I personally find self-remembering to be more difficult. However, as it is when succeeding in any difficult task, it brings a wonderful feeling when you manage it, even for a short time.

Charles T. Tart, in his book, *Open Mind, Discriminating Mind,* says: "I have attempted to practice a kind of mindfulness, what Gurdjieff called self-remembering, for some years. Its value has been to help me become more fully and realistically aware of the world around me and of the workings of my own mind."

Tart then describes the process very simply: "Self-remembering involves deliberately splitting your attention into two parts. The ordinary part gets involved in the usual way in what is happening in your world and your reaction to it. The extraordinary part monitors the first part in a *nonjudgmental* way, producing genuine self-consciousness: an awareness of being aware.

"Self-remembering can lead to many insights about the automatic, semiconscious aspects of our mental functioning of both cognition and emotion, and are able to function in a less automatic, more intelligent way."

Charles Tart has written an enlightening book of Gurdjieff's ideas in which he goes into more detail about self-remembering. If you want to go further into Gurdjieff's work, Charles Tart is a reliable guide.

I haven't tried to understand Gurdjieff's ideas of the universe and our place in it, any more than I have tried to assimilate his theory of octaves and vibrations, but even without tackling these esoteric theories, Gurdjieff gives me plenty to work on.

A Journal entry in the spring of 1980 reveals the hold that Gurdjieff still has on me: *Gurdjieff pervades my life these days, telling me things the Zen people have told me, and the Tibetans, but telling me somehow in a different way, for instance, "Don't be hurt by hostility, try to understand it" And now I try that.*

Gurdjieff didn't want to be viewed as a father figure. He didn't want to be a cult leader or a guru, he wanted his students to question everything, accept nothing on faith, but he had little patience. He was often cruel, enigmatic, or disappointing to his pupils, and he dismissed even the most loyal when he felt it was time they confronted the world on their own. But once in a while he said something comforting. I like to remember that he told a group, "This is difficult work, but you are not doing it for yourself alone, you are doing it for all humanity."

At first I didn't understand this, but I can see it more clearly now I realize that making myself a better, strong, more aware person will affect those around me and perhaps others through them.

There are several of Gurdjieff's suggestions I try to follow. One is to do a difficult thing every day. Sometimes my "difficult thing" is just walking a bit farther than I really want to, but often it is something unpleasant like preparing the income tax form. Once in a while I am faced with something truly difficult that I must handle somehow.

Gurdjieff taught that we should not listen to negative thoughts. Ouspensky said, "Energy is wasted on unnecessary and unpleasant emotions, on the expectation of unpleasant things possible or impossible, on bad moods, on unnecessary haste, nervousness, irritability and day dreams, etc."

Ouspensky was as strict a teacher as Gurdjieff himself. I knew that often an event or even a book I've read hasn't felt real to me until I have described it to someone. Ouspensky doesn't approve of this. "It is very difficult for a man to keep silent about things that interest him. He would like to speak about them to everyone with whom he is accustomed to sharing his thoughts, as he calls it. This is the most difficult abstinence of all. . . . Only a man who can be silent when necessary can be master of himself."

Another Ouspensky remark struck home: "It is very useful to try to struggle with the habit of giving immediate expression to all one's unpleasant emotions."

One more Gurdjieff rule that I try to follow is to break a habit, any habit. I do this from time to time, though only small habits, like skipping the glass of sherry I like to have before dinner every night, or, though I like a nap after lunch, I often go without it.

One last Gurdjieff item. About ten years ago I made up a list I headed A FEW GURDJIEFF SUGGESTIONS FOR WORKING ON ONESELF and I put it in my current journal, moving it each time I begin a new one. There are about fourteen items, several of which I have already described to you. I'll list a few of the others:

Stop the flow of aimless chatter in your mind.

Meditate daily, reminding yourself why you are doing this work.

Relax any muscle not in use at the moment.

See your surroundings clearly.

Try to pinpoint your chief fault.

Observe yourself.

This is all, at least for now, about Gurdjieff. I hope you have realized that he was an odd but sensible man. I found him a great challenge and tried to follow his orders. Then, finally, I made this entry in my journal:

Something, more likely someone, (Gurdjieff, Aldous Huxley?) has made me begin to place everyday attitudes and reactions against the larger scale of eternity, of this life and what's next, or what really matters, of a person's well-being or equilibrium.

This has made a great difference in my supporting the complications of Fred's illness. I put a TV program on the news in its proper perspective—it can be missed—and hours for meals are not important—they can be juggled—while doing the jigsaw puzzle with Fred is not now a "waste of time." It soothes him.

And it also puts into proper perspective my pull toward the typewriter—it's an indulgence but of no importance. I could go on forever about Gurdjieff and Ouspensky, but I must change the subject.

Though learning to have a better perspective on my situation was an improvement, I knew that I could use more help. I remembered the time, not far in the past, when I had blindly stepped off into space at the head of the stairs, and I thought I might be whistling in the dark when I let myself think I was doing better.

I had been reading John Lilly's books about the dolphins being studied in Florida. From his description it seemed as if the dolphins were often one jump ahead of humans, and I remember wishing I could make friends with a dolphin.

Then somewhere I read that John Lilly had two spirits who kept an eye on him—protected him, he thought.

And I thought to myself, a spirit could be a good friend, maybe better than a dolphin. John Lilly had two masculine spirits, but I thought I'd like a woman one too, so I imagined, pretended, almost believed that two spirits were in the atmosphere above and behind my head, silently watching over me. It was a comforting thought. I never called on my invisible friends for help, though through most of those difficult years, I felt they were not far away. Probably the combination of being, however remotely, protected, steadied me.

Astonishingly, the other day, here in Sonoma, California, I found my protectors had not forgotten me, though I had forgotten them.

The wonderful award I told you about in the first chapter had just come, making me feel my life and my work had real value. I was so elated by this unexpected recognition that, out in the garden—I think I was hanging up clothes to dry—while I was listening to the birds singing their hearts out and everything was so green after the rains, I smelled the lilac blossoms and admired a golden line of yellow iris. I was then swept with the feeling that life was so good to me, everything so glorious, that this would be the best time for me to die. Better to die, at eighty-seven, when the world was being so good to me, than to linger and go downhill in my old age. (I imagine I was unconsciously thinking of my poor mother.) I knew I wouldn't do anything to bring about my death, but I also knew if it happened, I'd welcome it.

That afternoon I was driving home from the Sonoma post office when unexpectedly I felt surrounded by love, the love of all my friends. I felt warm and cherished. It was a heavenly feeling, one I had never had before. Then, to my surprise, for I had long ago forgotten about them, I realized that my Vermont spirit-friends were in the atmosphere above and behind me. I kept driving, of course, and I don't know why I wasn't more surprised, but I said to them (silently) "You're there! Well, I'm ready if this is the time!"

They answered the same way, silently, but I heard them clearly, "It's not time yet. *It's too soon.*" They repeated this, "It's too soon."

So I drove home, thinking I knew that they were telling me that I still had a long way to go. I was wondering if I was to reach one hundred like my mother, and I added to myself, "It's probably not going to be an easy ending." I hoped my protectors would be handy when I needed them. I rather thought they would be.

But later, when I thought about my exalted feeling that this would be a good time to die, I could see that it was sheer *hubris* on my part. I had thought of the cry of the Indian braves when they were going into battle, shouting, "This is a good day to die!"

I knew, of course, I didn't belong in that august company of strong, brave people. I must still have a lot to learn. I will work at learning it.

Now I am going on to tell you about a very different person, though Gurdjieff would have approved of her, I'm sure. I'm going to tell you about my first cousin, Emily Rockwood, who lived to within two months of one hundred and two. On the day she died, she was still following her own road, one that was very different from most of the people she lived among, in an old people's home. She was born inner-directed. Mary Austin would have liked her. And so will you, I hope.

SUMMING UP: If you get your library to find Ouspensky's book, or de Hartmann's, you will find they read almost like novels, yet give you a great deal of potent information.

CHAPTER EIGHT

✒

"You're Not Old Until You're Ninety"

I HAVE WANTED TO TELL YOU ABOUT Emily Rockwood from the moment I began this book. She was a beacon in front of me, a light to follow. She had so much spirit, so much humor and she saw herself so clearly.

But first I had to read over her letters. We had begun a lively correspondence after she entered an old people's home, "The Inn," in Florida, when she was eighty-five.

I found I had about fifty letters from her, written in her strong, rounded handwriting—no grade school Palmer Method for Emily! When, later, she couldn't see what she was writing, her penciled uneven letters still gave out the rich flavor of her indomitable spirit.

Emily Rockwood was born in January, 1883. She died in December, 1984. A fortunate woman, she was her (feisty) self to the end.

In the summer of 1971, Emily Rockwood and her good friend, Jessie, had been asked to look after a beautiful little house perched above the sea in Rockport on the rugged New England coast. (Emily often escaped from The Inn to visit Jessie and twice escaped for the entire summer.)

It seems a pleasant coincidence to remember that Emily was then exactly the age I am as I write this, eighty-eight.

When I drove to Rockport, I didn't know it was to be the last time I would see her. I hadn't seen her for several years and I was pleased to find she had retained much of her strength and all of her quick mind. She didn't seem to have changed at all; it was characteristic of her to say as she got slowly up from a low chair, "It's only my body that gives me trouble. It creaks and it cracks, but it's not me. I only live in it."

Then she gave me a straight look. "I see you've finally grown up. How do you enjoy your white hair?" I was sixty-five then, and I didn't think of myself as old. In fact, I hadn't realized my hair was white; I thought it was still grey. But Emily hadn't finished. "You might try a cane," she was saying. "The combination gets me all sorts of privileges."

(I must confess I differ from Emily in many ways and this is one of them. Although I have fallen from time to time, I rarely use a cane, and I'm so stiff-necked I don't want special privileges because I'm old.)

Emily Rockwood was my first cousin, her mother the older sister of my mother. I remember being told that my grandmother had had her last child, her eleventh, as her oldest daughter was having her first, Emily. Times have changed, haven't they?

I didn't see Emily often while I was growing up, but when, at twenty, I summoned the daring to board a commuter train to Jersey City from my home in Cranford, to catch the ferry to Manhattan, my life changed.

I had gotten a job in Greenwich Village on a new magazine, *Plain Talk*, one my mother considered a "muckraker," though I thought it a trailblazer. My mother didn't approve of my working in New York.

It wasn't long before my mother reminded me that her sister, my aunt, who was living on East 56th Street, would be glad to put me up for the night, if I had to work late. I understood right away why she had made this suggestion.

About once a week I had found it convenient to spend the night in the city, and on those occasions I stayed with Doris, a good friend who had rented a basement apartment in Greenwich Village. The front window in her bedroom had a grating over it, and through it you could see the steps leading down to the apartment, and also the feet walking by on the sidewalk above.

Doris was very hospitable and I loved staying there, particularly as our sleep was often interrupted by one of her friends (usually male) tapping on the window, mouthing through it, "You *can't* be asleep this early!" Doris always let the visitor in and then got back in bed, while her friend filled her in on the latest publishing gossip. (I was sitting up in the other bed, wide-eyed.) This behavior seemed marvelously bohemian to me, but I never should have told my mother about it. To placate her, I followed her suggestion, staying the night with my aunt from time to time. I found I enjoyed that fully as much, though in a different way from the risqué delights of Greenwich Village.

My cousin, Emily, about forty at the time, was very busy running an interior decorating shop on the street floor of her family's brownstone house. The shop always glowed with color. Delicate, dazzling fabrics—gold tissue, vivid cretonnes printed with wild flowers—were strewn over the chairs and sofas. When I was married two years later, Emily's wedding present to me was a knife-pleated, Fortuny, sea-green tissue gown that clung like skin to my body, right down to my ankles, turning me into a mermaid. I am ashamed to admit that in those days my body embarrassed me. I never wore that lovely ethereal gown and I don't even remember to whom I finally gave it. (If it still exists, it's probably in a museum.)

I wonder what you would have made of Emily if you had met her then. She was plain, which as we all know, is a curse for a woman in our culture. Her nose tilted up and her face always looked recently scrubbed. Emily's straight black hair was pulled back into a knob on the curve of her head. Her body was spare but straight as an arrow.

Emily had already developed a faculty for being comfortable with people of any age. She never made me feel that she was older than I. She had not married but was always ready to hear about my dates and interests, which were just then centering on one person.

Emily supported herself with her shop and, I suspect, helped her father and mother financially. To escape the unbearable heat of New York summers, she rented a small shingled fisherman's cottage on the edge of the beautiful beach at Ogunquit, Maine, where she carried on a flourishing business. She took her mother up with her and twice asked me to visit them there. (Emily spoke of this many years later in one of those letters from Florida, reminding me that my one-piece bathing suit with no skirt had shocked her mother.)

When her father and mother grew old, Emily moved them to Florida, and after they left her, Emily stayed on, making summer forays north with her friend, Jessie, usually house-sitting for vacationing friends. When she was finally too old to remain totally independent, she entered "The Inn," a home for elderly people. Her graphic letters describing her life there gave me a series of pictures that astonished me. In that unlikely atmosphere she retained her cheerful spirit and her caustic wit, and even her relish for life itself.

Emily described the birds and flowering trees that surrounded her when she worked in her garden, so when she wrote, "I must be a comical sight, tending my garden with one hand and hanging on to my cane with the other!" I could see Emily standing awkwardly, cane in one hand, rake in the other, clearing the leaves away from her little flower bed, while birds sang around her.

If you are surprised to find her working in her garden at an old people's home, this was the result of her own magic. She had persuaded the director to let her have a little patch of ground to cultivate, just below her window.

She had two windows in her room, always crowded with seedlings and pots of blossoming flowers. Her room was ten feet by ten feet, and she used every inch of it. When the other old ladies looked in on her, they laughed, she said. And I could imagine a prim old woman looking around, saying, "What a clutter!"

But Emily said, "It's the only place I have, so why shouldn't it be full? My interests don't shrink with age, though my ability to do things does! I like to have my different baskets on the floor, handy to my chair—and all my books, of course." She didn't mention the trowel, the little rake and the watering can she kept handy, too. She was always working on something. "At present, I am hooking a cushion for Jessie's cat, which proves how exciting are our interests here!"

Later, in 1976, she hooked a small rug for our Christmas. She was then ninety-three. She embroidered her initials and the year on the rug. It lies beside me now on my chaise lounge and I admire the beautiful red flower at the bottom. I like to think Emily liked that red flower, too.

Once she wrote that when a person died at the Inn, all their possessions were tossed out. She asked me if I would like any of her "trashy treasures," and when I answered I'd be honored to have them, she sent me a picture of herself at sixteen, with her two small brothers. (She looked prim and very much in charge.) She also sent a daguerreotype of her mother in her youth, who already had the sweet patient look I remembered. With these priceless pictures came one of our mutual great-grandmother, Hester Levy. I had never seen a photograph of her before; she was a strikingly handsome woman. These were treasures indeed, and far from "trashy."

I had always thought that Emily's life had not been an easy one, brought up strictly as she was, having to support herself throughout her life, never enjoying the frivolous amusements most of us have had. I always admired her cheerfulness and courage. But I found out that Emily did not see her life as I did. This emerged from an encounter with the chaplain at the Inn.

I imagine the conversation took place in her little room, the chaplain moving cautiously among the baskets and books spread over the floor. Emily wrote, "The chaplain here is a nice man, but he says I stress fun too much. That is because there is so little of it here! Maybe he has had less of it than I have had, which makes me miss it." I am sure Emily got the better of the nice chaplain in that encounter, but he wasn't the only one to criticize her. "There are those who say I am a bad woman, but don't you believe them!"

This was probably because she had never given up her love for a cigarette. How Emily managed to cajole the people at the Inn into indulging her in the pernicious habit of smoking would have been hard for me to understand if I'd not long ago discovered Emily usually got what she wanted. Even when she was in her nineties, she would be taken out to the garden in her wheelchair for the pleasure of smoking her one cigarette of the day.

My younger readers may not know that doctors often recommend to their elderly patients a glass of wine before dinner and Emily's letter on this subject made me break into laughter.

Emily was reporting on her 89th birthday, "my last birthday before old age. After my next, the 90th, I can no longer claim to be even elderly." She went on, "Jessie came to visit and we had a good time, if a quiet one. We had parties in my room. Birthday cake and sherry. Jessie had given me a gallon bottle of sherry for Christmas," (It was that Christmas gift that made me laugh.) Emily went on, "It amuses outsiders to think of all the old women indulging in drink. I guess they all do. There was one who went too far in her indulgence. It was so particularly hushed up that everyone knew about it."

Emily saw herself very clearly and did not pretend to feelings she didn't have. "This Inn is a cross-section of a woman's world. Everything from a club-woman type to a family cast-off." (She never minced words!) "When I'm good-natured, I find it amusing, but some days I'm disgruntled and don't. But life runs along smoothly with the simple pleasures of second childhood." And she added, always aware of what was going on outside her small world, "Hope you're not snowed in and freezing way up there in Vermont. We're in the midst of our first cold spell. I have been busily covering the flowers in my garden against tonight's frost."

I keep smiling as I read her letters. "I assure you old age is a strange condition, but one can take more than one would think," she wrote me. I can say Amen to that!

When she was ninety-seven, her nephew and his wife came by to take her out to dinner. "So you can see things are looking up! What I pay for fun is little compared to what it does for me. Why should I mind lying in bed after a good time? The payment for my gay actions struck me all of a sudden, but the fun was worth it."

A little later on, "I'm not a nice old lady at all. Yesterday I had to speak pleasantly to the dentist, though I would have preferred to bite his fingers." I respond to that too!

I find that most people don't like to think about death, but Emily often spoke of it. I remember in 1971 when we were visiting her I spoke of my mother who was then ninety-seven.

Emily said with conviction, "The nearer you get to the end of your life, the less you mind the thought of death."

I think I said, "It's just a change."

She answered cheerfully, "For the better!"

Later in the same year she wrote me again: "Death is my next great adventure and I welcome it. The last days have been hard to take, not being able to do anything and lacking patience to accept it. Maybe I will improve."

She had nearly five more years to go, but she must have had death often in her mind, for she wrote about it again, "Dying is my next step. After that I believe something good comes and I pray it will be a busy time, working. I am bored with doing nothing, and learning nothing. I am bored with my ignorance about so much."

Her spirit, her courage, her clarity, her humor, never lessened as she grew older. You may remember that she said, "My interests do not shrink with age." Instead of growing less aware, less observant, less interested in the world around her and the world outside of it, Emily remained alert and interested in everything. Though she often mentioned casually being in and out of the hospital, she never mentioned operations or physical symptoms.

We always called Emily on her birthday. I have come upon a note in my journal, *January 29, 1982: Today is Emily*

Rockwood's 99th birthday. I called the Inn yesterday to set up a phone call, so this morning she was stationed in a wheelchair by the phone and when we called, she answered the phone herself! After the Happy Birthdays and good wishes, Emily said, "You may laugh at me but I am worried about you all and earthquakes. The TV stresses unpleasant things and I hate to think of such following you to your new house." I reassured her and she added, "Old age encourages worries!"

I had to dry my eyes after I talked to her. She sounded frail but very clear in her mind.

I had made a friend of the manager at the Inn, so I wrote her in 1984, as Emily's eyesight had forced her to stop writing. I was cheered by the reply that came back. "She is out in her wheelchair daily, smoking and enjoying the outdoors—still alert—and feisty most of the time— eats well—sleeps well—no pain—her eyesight is poor— hearing is fine." She was then 101.

My friend wrote me later that Emily had died, as she had lived, with grace. She had been taken out into the garden for a cigarette after lunch, had returned to take a nap and, while sleeping, left us.

You can't be surprised that Emily has been my role model for years. I am still in my own home, hoping to keep out of any and all "Health Centers," hoping that if I have to enter one, I will take it as cheerfully as Emily. I remember her letter, "Unfortunately, I am again in the Health Center, if very unwillingly. It cramps my style unmercifully, but I am beginning to feel better, if not younger."

I sometimes wonder whether Emily Rockwood would approve of my present interests and experiments. I rather imagine she would have been puzzled, if not downright antagonistic, to the idea of controlling one's mind and one's body. I suspect Mrs. Wheelock would have agreed with her. Better to tend to the natural things of life, growing things, watching the seasons, "traveling through the woods in the spring." Those two would have enjoyed each other.

As for Gurdjieff, he certainly would have approved of Emily Rockwood, who did more than one difficult thing every day of her life, even in old age, and had no illusions about herself. She didn't need Gurdjieff to tell her to be aware of her weaknesses.

SUMMING UP: Let's let Emily Rockwood have a last provocative word. She once wrote me, "It's a shame to confess it but I do not make a good job of being an old woman," and then added, "Do you suppose I expected to live forever?" As to the first remark, if I can make as good a job of being an old woman as Emily, I'll be surprised and delighted. As for expecting to live forever, I don't, and the way it takes me is to make me feel in a hurry to get done all I want to do while I'm still here. (I'm already making notes for the autobiography I'll start as soon as this book is launched.)

∅

CHAPTER NINE

Strange Experiences in California

I T SEEMED LIKE A MIRACLE when a New York specialist put his finger on the exact cause of Fred's arthritis—and cured it! We were no longer entangled with hospitals and doctors. As I told you earlier we were able to take the great leap; we moved to California in 1977.

We left Vermont because our two sons, both of whom were settled in California, used the irresistible argument that they wanted our grandchildren to know us. So we uprooted, not entirely unwillingly. The deep snow and bitter cold in Vermont had made their own argument. (I've just come upon a note in my journal: *When you are in your seventies, and the thermometer says it is eight degrees below zero outside, you don't forget it for a minute.* (I was seventy-two that winter.)

The climate wasn't the only appeal that California had for me, for I still believed that every new place offered not only challenges but opportunities. We were used to moving, of course, and I remembered that in the Foreign

Service we had to learn a new language at almost every post; in California we wouldn't have that particular challenge, though I realize now I have picked up some additions to my vocabulary, "laid back," "flaky", "funky," etc.

I was full of hope when we got off the plane in San Francisco. I was sure Fred would feel well in "sunny" California. It was Christmas time and we celebrated with our two families. All the signs looked good. I plunged into work, hoping to complete a book I was writing about our life abroad. I didn't have a workroom in our rented house, but I set up my typewriter in my bedroom. I located the town library and found a friendly bookstore, and I went back to reading the collected letters of Aldous Huxley which I had begun in Vermont. (I had developed an odd affinity with Huxley.)

That spring I was bothered by a sore throat that wouldn't go away; it finally moved into a serious case of the flu. You may be surprised to hear that, though I had a high temperature with all the usual aches and distresses, I remember that particular case of flu almost fondly. Afterwards I felt as if another and beautiful world was so close to ours it could be experienced under special circumstances. Months later I realized that having that flu had made me better able to accept phenomena like the imaginary doctor and even that fleeting glimpse of myself as beautiful.

The high temperature gave me a constant stream of extraordinary images, so comforting and pleasant that, in a coherent moment, I asked Fred to bring me my cassette recorder.

I have just listened to that tape and found it a strange experience: the whispering voice, the long deep sighs and once or twice a rueful laugh. (I later transcribed the tape; it came to eight pages.)

The tape begins:

All these visions, colors, scenes, weigh on me, as if I were responsible for recording this strange experience. I wonder why this illness is so visual. Is it from some chemical I've been taking?

I closed my eyes just now and saw I was under a huge arched ceiling, rounded like an Eskimo hut, but a story-and-a-half high. The whole ceiling was embroidered in soft designs and symbols. The great expanse of floor was empty. There was no one there. I heard my voice saying, I am alone; I wish I weren't alone!

Another feverish day: I found I was playing by a tidal pool with someone like me. We were idly dipping our hands into the brown-green water, then letting it drip off. I said, "I wonder what sea this is." The other one said, "The Irish Sea, I should think."

We saw little thin-skinned brown crabs in the water and I wondered if they'd mind if I picked one up. I was confident no creature would harm me. The little crab, its puffy paperlike skin so fragile, moved timidly around my hand.

The place we were in was lovely — the edge of a long, low, rocky shore, the sea grey-blue. Air and salt and space. Not a factory, pier or airplane.

And then I added: The strange country of high temperature is very different from dreams; it seems to focus on beautiful, empty landscapes.

I often think about that experience; who was the "someone like me"? Was she the friend whom I kept looking for? I hope that some day I will come upon that "Irish Sea," so peaceful and beautiful.

When I was better, I resumed reading Huxley's letters and to my delight and surprise I came upon:

"I stupidly went and got a virus two weeks ago, was in bed four or five days with a temperature. . . . Some kind of vague imagery starts with me, at about one hundred and two. . . . The images become progressively more vivid as the fever mounts above that point."

It seems strange that I have always felt Huxley was my true friend. I dreamed about him about a year later (April 23, 1979).

Last night in a dream, I had a conversation with Aldous Huxley. I said to him, "Don't forget you're going to help me when I die, help me get through the difficult part." And Aldous Huxley answered, "Yes, I am ready, if you need me. But you have two protectors, you know!"

"Two protectors? Do I?"

"Yes, they've been with you for some time now."

I had an image of two large, cloud-like figures hovering above me. How comforting!

I had forgotten that I had acquired those "protectors" in Vermont, but when I realized Aldous Huxley accepted them, I thought I might be able to depend on them to help me in a crisis. However, as it turned out, I forgot them again. They surprised me by surfacing a few years later, as I have already told you.

I don't know when I got the idea that Aldous Huxley would meet me when I died. Wishful thinking, of course. I think it must have been when I read the Tibetan *Book of the Dead*, with its frightening figures that are really just an aspect of one's self, they say. Huxley would be a stalwart companion through that fearsome introduction to death, (if the Tibetans do know something we don't know.)

I seemed to be continually in trouble those first months in California. The flu behind me, almost at once I sprained my ankle, struggling along with crutches for a week or two.

Finally well again, I was free to concentrate on the work in hand, I went back to the Foreign Service book and on June 9th I put two exclamation points beside the date. I had finished the first draft of my book.

511 pages, 120,000 words. How it must be cut! I can't wait to get back at it, really writing it, but how will I manage to find time to work on it for the months it will take?

Then on August 28th, a real disaster struck. My husband had a severe stroke.

I didn't write in my journal for ten days.

September 8, 1978 : Of course the whole thing, Fred having been so near to dying, makes me know solidly, as a fact, that he will die, and probably before me. I also know that our life probably is forever changed, that he may never be able to drive the car again, that I must handle everything from here on; this is hard to swallow. The trip to Mendocino canceled. The trip to Salt Lake canceled. Our visit to John and his family canceled. Even making a place for ourselves in Sonoma won't work out.

My first thought on realizing this great change was for my book, but I am going to try to be detached enough to hold a part of my mind steady and cool. Perhaps I can think about it when I'm rested and Fred is better. I might be able to work early in the morning.

That entry finished without punctuation and the next entry is almost a month later:

6 AM I'm nearly overwhelmed by the prospect of the coming day. But at last I have the energy to walk again. I make the time by going about 8 A.M. when Fred has had his breakfast and gone back to sleep. (Today I met a man I have often met on my walks. Today he said, "And where is your partner?" I only smiled, but the question echoed all day in my mind.)

As for my book, I rely on Gurdjieff to help me realize it is not important. The Zen people would say it is an "attachment," to be shucked off. I'm not ready to shuck off my "attachments," but I can understand why they have no importance.

These are heavy days.

My seventy-third birthday is behind me.

It took two years to finish the revision of my book.

Thus our introduction to Sonoma turned out to be a repeat of Bennington. The big difference between our experience in Vermont and California was that both our sons and their families were within driving distance and were an immense support. However, I had already learned that in such situations, it is one's own strength and endurance that counts. I looked for that strength in my own way, doing my relaxation exercises twice a day and reading my books. Whenever I could, I worked on the revision on the book I was calling *Forever A Stranger*.

Was it because my life was so restricted that my meditations were more rewarding than ever before? The images that arose before my closed eyes; the overflowing deep blue pool, the tiny brightly sunlit landscapes far away, and once, the face of a man, so alive and seemingly breathing that I described him in my journal:

I saw a man's head in full color, as vivid as an illustration in a magazine. I could even see, faintly, the pores in his skin. He was looking toward me but not at me. He had smooth short brown hair, blue eyes, and a ruddy complexion. He was full of life and confidence. He looked like a successful stockbroker or an ad man. I had never seen him before. I saw him clearly and then he vanished, leaving nothing behind.

About that time I came upon a new book by Mike Samuels, this one written with his wife, Nancy. Mike Samuels was the author of *The Well Body Book*, which I still was finding very helpful. I was working one of their visualization exercises in which I imagined I saw a white flag flying against a pale blue sky and then, following instructions, changed the color of the flag to red, then yellow, black, etc. If you've never tried visualization, it is a good training exercise.

But the new book took me even further. *Seeing With the Mind's Eye: The History, Techniques and Uses of Visualization* is beautifully illustrated with provocative photographs. I learned a great deal from it. It is so full of meat, actual exercises, discussions and illustrations that I can't do justice to it here. However, I copied out for myself some of the most intriguing chapter headings. Here are a few:

Strengthening Confidence; Visualizing Yourself; Drifting in Space; Rehearsing a Talk; If You Want a Material Thing; Self-Healing, Autogenic Exercises, etc. It's an exciting book.

To get back to my own situation, at the time I was again looking for all the help I could get. In many ways Fred's stroke hadn't incapacitated him as much as that devilish arthritis in Vermont, for he was able to go with me to visit our sons for the weekend and to have them here. Nevertheless, he had lost most of his energy and of course left everything to me, even letting me find a house we could buy in 1979, so I had to talk to real estate agents and look at possible houses, a role very foreign to me. There were times when it all seemed almost too much for me, but instead of stepping off into space at the top of the stairs, as I had done in Vermont, I found an unexpected comfort. It developed out of my new interest in visualization.

I had often tried to interest Fred in the new skill I was attempting as I thought visualization might help him, but he didn't believe in any of it. We had a conversation that distressed me. I recorded it sadly in my journal.

Fred was talking about reading health journals, about strokes and cholesterol. "It's so depressing to read about your arteries and your heart and all," he said.

I: "But it's not depressing if you're learning how to keep them in good shape."

"Oh, I hate even thinking about my insides. I always hated physiology and my family, being Christian Scientists, told me I shouldn't try to learn that stuff."

"But your body is so marvelous. It goes along all day and all night, doing things for you and you don't even have to tell it what to do. I've been trying to be conscious that my heart is beating. Do you ever hear your heart beat?"

"No, never. And I don't want to."

I changed the subject. It seemed sad to me that he feels that way about his body, as if he were housed in something disgusting, that he tries to ignore.

I think of my body as a good friend and I try to cooperate with it, to help it keep me well. And I like to hear that 73-year-old heart pounding cheerfully away!

It was the morning after this conversation when I was desperately trying to understand the realtor's jargon about mortgages and titles and termites that, while Fred was taking a nap, I realized I simply had to pull myself together, I must not let myself be overwhelmed by Fred's frail condition and the responsibility of finding the right house. I felt I could easily break down and cry hysterically. I recorded in my journal how I warded off this attack of self-pity:

Today I tried a new gimmick. I lay down and pictured myself inside an enclosure made by a high rosemary hedge like the one we had had around our place in my childhood. The enclosure reminded me of the tapestry of the unicorn inside a circular fence that I'd seen once in a New York museum.

I turned on warm sunlight. I lay first on a cot covered with a fur robe, then lay on the grass so as to feel the earth beneath me. I felt that the sky with the planets, the stars and the moon and the sun were raining their energy down on me. I smelt sweet daphne nearby and when I opened my eyes I saw the beautiful thick green hedge, dotted with flat-petalled pale pink roses. I lay there for twenty minutes. I felt rather dizzy when I got up, but rested.

That entry was March 6, 1990. The next one is dated March 9th. I had been doing the same visualization every day apparently. The March 9th entry begins in a rather startling way:

Now I have the unicorn with me in my flower-dotted green enclosure. He leapt gracefully over the hedge, then came close to me, settling down beside my cot where I lie stretched out on my back, the sun full on me, warm and bright.

He is pure ivory-white, the same color as his horn. Only his tiny hoofs are a polished black.

He likes me to rub the base of his horn and ears. When he turns toward me, he is careful not to poke me with his sharp horn.

Once I tried riding on him. He didn't mind. He moved around the ring with me as if we'd done this every day, but I thought I must be too heavy for his slight frame, so I haven't tried again.

Have I given him a name, you ask? No. He has no name for me, therefore I have none for him. It would be rather like calling someone by his first name when he is still being formal with you. So, I feel, it is with this sweet unicorn.

This entry was the only mention of the unicorn, but I can remember to this day what a comforting presence he was, and though I didn't record it, I am sure that during those difficult days I often lay on that sunny cot, with my hand resting on the soft, white fur of the little unicorn.

Visualization is such a mysterious power. As you know, I had already benefited from it through Jaime, my "imaginary doctor," who continues to give me good, though often unwelcome, advice.

I'd like to make it clear that those were difficult days, when I summoned up the unicorn for comfort and consolation, but even then I realized that I had become more in control of myself than before. As early as December, 1979, I had written:

I guess every writer has a secret life, perhaps every woman. I hug mine to me: my private files, my special friends, the light I saw during my meditation today—before I was interrupted by a call from Fred. "Where is everybody?" And my early morning walks.

Sometimes I wonder how it would be if my secret life were my real life, if I could have had time to follow through on my ideas to have the privacy and quiet to go further.

But I am lucky to have evolved to this point. At noon today I fell asleep and dreamt that I was angry and that old familiar demon screamed and complained, the demon who used to hold me quite often, years ago, but no more. And when I saw that angry little woman, in my dream I smiled as I recognized her and, waking, thought, "Poor little thing! She is one of the 'I's deep inside of me; she needs love and I must give it to her."

I think now about that "angry little woman." I wonder if I should try to find her again. Is she still angry?

SUMMING UP: As is evident in this chapter, visualization is a very useful tool. Everyone should try it! You may not be blessed with the company of a unicorn, but every step you take along the way, however hesitantly, will open up new horizons.

CHAPTER TEN

♋

Curiouser and Curiouser

T HEN ANOTHER BOOK EXPLODED ACROSS MY PATH. I am not sure exactly when this was, probably about 1980. I had read accounts of a new technique that was being called "biofeedback." It sounded interesting so when I saw *Beyond Biofeedback* on a shelf in the library I picked it up. When I'd read it, I bought a copy so I could read it over and over.

The word *beyond* is the clue to the book. It goes way beyond biofeedback. It begins beyond anything I had ever heard seriously discussed. I had never run across a reputable scientist who, commenting on Dr. Rhine's early experiments with ESP had said more than, "interesting, but . . ."

Beyond Biofeedback is by Elmer and Alyce Green. It has two aspects. It is a report of their experiments in body control; that is, their control of the autonomic (involuntary) components of our bodies—at a time that I hadn't yet heard of any scientist rash enough to even theorize on that subject!—and it is also a fascinating account of the life of these two scientists.

The scientific sections were not easy for me to follow and I didn't try very hard. I raced through the book as if it were a novel; I couldn't put it down.

Here was a scientist who was also psychic and who married another scientist-psychic. (Her story is as absorbing as his.)

In reading the book, I also came upon other interesting people whose books I searched out: Rolling Thunder, Doug Boyd, and Uri Geller.

I made an entry in my journal on November 17, 1982, that expressed how I felt about this book:

Elmer and Alyce Green's Beyond Biofeedback *has convinced me that, even without a guide and the machinery of feedback, I can benefit from the autogenic exercises. I am going to try to do them twice a day for half an hour. Of course I can't do that every day, Thanksgiving weekend, for instance, but I've already begun the new regime.*

Two weeks later I enlarged on the effect the book had on me.

I am doing the autogenic exercises as regularly as possible. I put a sign on my door, CONCENTRATING, just to be safe!

The Greens echo so many people: Mary Austin, Gurdjieff, William James, John Lilly, Carlos Castaneda. It's as if the Greens had summed up and made respectable all the far-out ideas I have been reading for years with hope—and doubt. I began with James, or was it Alexandra David-Neel? Never mind who it was!

I intend to work hard on myself. The Greens reintroduced me to the idea of "field dependent" and "field independent" I have always been so "field dependent," conscious of how other people regarded me, how they see me, that it has practically paralyzed me.

In the last few years I have gained a small measure of independence by working on myself and in insisting on a place to write, but often when I listened to my thoughts I noticed they are centered on the impression I am making on other people. On the Bike Path, if someone is coming toward me, I walk more vigorously, hoping they will think, "That's quite an old woman to be walking so fast!" and I even hope someone will ask how far I am walking, so I can answer with false modesty. "Only four miles." And then I hastily catch myself and begin again my habitual Tibetan chant, Om Mani Padme Hum" which I am using to quiet my mind.

(As I read that now, I am thinking that at least Gurdjieff would at least have been pleased that I was aware of my foolish thoughts—Self Observation!)

I still enjoy the Greens' book immensely, reading it again from time to time, but its real value has been, not only in making me feel that control of our bodies is really possible, but in the detailed exercises that I can easily follow.

There's one more thing I must tell you: I was astonished to find the Greens accepted Carlos Castaneda's books as an important contribution. Up till then, I had read only scoffing comments on his work. As you may remember, in Vermont I was mesmerized by Carlos Castaneda, believing and not believing, but trying some of his suggestions, especially his way of writing his books by "dreaming" them. It sounded so easy! (I have never been able to do this, though every so often I feel I'm on the edge, as when a meditation solves a problem for me, or on waking from sleep, I am given a solution to a puzzling tangle in my writing.)

The Greens refer to Castaneda all through their book. I was so impressed by one quote that I typed it for myself in 1981. As this passage relates to what I have been trying to do—change my ways and break useless habits—perhaps you too will find it interesting:

"If a person decided to modify a habit, it seems that everything conspires to prevent change. Don Juan explained this to Carlos Castaneda when Carlos was trying to develop 'lucid dreaming,' trying to become fully aware of being himself in his dreams. . . . In *Tales of Power*, Carlos tells how don Juan warned him that the early state of developing this ability consisted of 'a deadly game that one's mind played itself, and that some part of myself was going to do everything to prevent the fulfillment of my task. That could include, don Juan had said, plunging me into a loss of meaning, melancholy, or even a suicidal depression. I did not go that far, however. My experience was rather on the light, comical side; nonetheless, the result was equally frustrating.'"

The Greens continued: "In other words, trying to make a psychological change is going to be opposed by the mind itself. Anyone who has tried to break a habit or change his ways knows about that.

"From the yogic point of view, psychological homeostasis represents not only a psychological state but also a physiological state. That is why fasting, diets, various physical exercises and emotional—and mental control—exercises are considered necessary or useful at the least, in bringing about personality change and development."

This reminded me of Gurdjieff, who did not explain why, but asked his followers to do difficult mental exercises, intricate dances, and almost impossible physical feats. Have you read Ouspensky? Once the STOP exercise was almost a killer when Gurdjieff's students were ordered to freeze when they heard Gurdjieff yell, "STOP!" One of them was working in an irrigation ditch that was slowly filling up. He froze. The water was reaching his chin when he heard Gurdjieff's voice from afar. "Enough!"

When you read this, you may decide to be a dilettante like me, but there are many stronger people who manage to break the "habit barrier" at least once. I am thinking of those people who have had a difficult time giving up smoking. (My own experience was prolonged but finally successful, in my sixties.)

By the time I chanced upon Elmer and Alyce Green in 1980, my life had improved. My husband was stronger, I had found a little house on the street where we had been renting—the movers simply pushed the piano up the street. We turned half of the new garage into an almost perfect workroom. So I had a quiet, private place with my books and files close at hand. I couldn't even hear the telephone ringing in the house. My husband and I agreed that I would work one full day a week; I chose Tuesday. It was wonderful. Fred would fix his own lunch and I'd take a sandwich out to my work room. Evenings, when I was always tired out, we would go out to dinner. No housekeeping on Tuesdays.

I got back to my book about our life abroad, almost as happy as I had been in my below-ground hideaway in New Hampshire. I didn't have the colorful striped nomad's ceiling, but my sons and friends had painted the whole room a pleasant blue the Sunday before we moved in. I painted the door Chinese red and put on it a brass knocker from Istanbul, a woman's hand, which seemed suitable. The walls have many of the same "ornaments" as Antrim, as well as others I've acquired since. One is a large black feather. I just measured it; it's ten-and-a-half inches long. I'll tell you about it later.

I'm assuming you haven't found a copy of *Beyond Biofeedback* yet, but even if you have, you might be interested to hear how an inquisitive but casual practitioner of the art of improving herself made out with the Greens' unusual exercises.

It was a good time to try them. I began with "Warming of the Hands." I don't suppose you would want to try this, but it was a challenge I couldn't resist. I sent away for a finger thermometer. As I kept records of the results, I have now stopped writing to search for them.

✍

I should have been a file clerk; I file everything! I have just pulled out a folder I call "Work on Myself" which I began in 1962. The first entries are sad, but they cheered up when I discovered Aldous Huxley in 1970. Now I've come upon a useful quotation from Rolling Thunder, dated June 15, 1982: "You don't have to speak aloud everything you think!" I still need to remember that.

✍

And here, at last, are the records of "Warming My Hands," eight pages. I can remember how excited I was when the thermometer arrived and I could begin. I made a short entry in my Journal:

January 25, 1983. I've gotten a finger thermometer to register heat in the hands; it is considered relaxation. A change of ten to fifteen degrees is expected at first. Yesterday I did twenty-five.

I enlarged on that "considered relaxation" a week later.

Elmer and Alyce Green believe that raising the temperature of one's hands has a beneficial effect on the whole body. It can cure high blood pressure, steady the heart and control headaches.

As I began this exercise my finger's temperature was usually between 68 and 70.

To summarize the totals reported in those eight pages: The thermometer rose twenty-four degrees four times; ten times it didn't reach ten; five times it didn't change at all, and then once, twenty-seven degrees.

You are probably more interested in how I did this than in all those figures, but I can't tell you. It is so mysterious! It seems as if I was simply thinking that the blood was running down my arms and into my hands. At first I used a tape I'd made of the Greens' "autogenic phrases," which told me to be quiet, to feel peaceful and that my hands were warm. This was repeated over and over again. But after a while I didn't need the tape and nowadays when I do it, I simply think my hands are getting warm. I discarded the thermometer long ago.

I have worked out my own formula, though I am not sure where I got it. Although twice a day I do exercises that incorporate warming the hands, I often warm them when I am waiting at a traffic light or in a doctor's office, and very often when I don't fall readily asleep at night, I warm my hands—and my feet if they're cold. My personal formula is: "I am at peace. My arms are heavy and my hands are warm." And my hands are instantly warm.

The reason I keep on doing this is because of what I reported in my journal of September 26, 1984:

I have just indulged myself by reading a little in Elmer and Alyce Greens' Beyond Biofeedback. The passage I read made me feel I should rely more on the effect of warming my hands twice a day. (Actually it doesn't always work well each time but it works always to some extent.) The Greens feel that this exercise adjusts the whole body and can clear up existing infections and weaknesses!

Now, over ten years later, it not only always works but just writing this has warmed my hands! Amazing!

The other exercise I tried, beside doing their autogenic relaxation exercises, was one the Greens call a yogic exercise. They also consider it an exercise in body consciousness. It is called "Traveling Through the Body."

In 1969 a colleague had told them he had met a yogi from India, Swami Rama, who claimed to be able to stop his pulse. The Greens, though fascinated by psychic powers, were first of all scientists; they wanted to test this feat in their laboratory. Swami Rama was not only ready, he was eager. You should read the account of this experiment yourself. It's marvelous, literally. I don't want to spoil your future pleasure by paraphrasing the account, so I won't.

Elmer Green described Swami Rama as a tall (six-feet-one) well-built man. He reminded Green of an "Italian Renaissance nobleman."

It was Swami Rama who told the Greens about "Traveling Through the Body" and then demonstrated it.

The yogi asked someone to lie down flat on the floor. With a wand, Swami Rama touched sixty-one different points on the person's body at fifteen-second intervals. The only instruction given was that the person visualize as clearly as possible the feeling of being *inside* the points as they were named: the forehead, the throat, the right shoulder, etc.

The Greens expected us to remember the sequential numbers when we did this exercise. I found, however, that I became confused as to where I was, where I should go next, and often forgot what number came next, so I still use a tape whenever I do it. Perhaps you will be able to remember better than I. (I made the tape from the chart in the book.)

As Elmer Green introduced this exercise, he remarked, "The effects of this exercise were always interesting and sometimes remarkable."

I can testify to that. In fact, the results which I had completely justify, in my opinion, Elmer Green's statement that "each section of the body is alive with a life of its own, with its own physical needs and emotions." To that, I would add *and memory.*

In my journal of March 5, 1983, I made a complete report of both my husband's and my experiences doing this exercise.

Fred's "Traveling Through the Body" is peopled by unexpected friends, some he hasn't seen since childhood, even the man who was town druggist of Groton, CT, in 1914! Sometimes he sees people in the news — Reagan, for instance — and he said that the other day Katy, his granddaughter, popped up by his big toe!

My "Travels" don't produce anything so spectacular, but as I focus my attention on each part, I get its history.

My right thumb remembers the comfortable feeling of being sucked when I was a child. (I sucked it long after my mother wished I'd stop; I even developed a callous on it.) My knees remember when I fell on the sidewalk in Rumson, N. J., and skinned them. My right ankle remembers when I stepped into a rabbit hole on the edge of Carnegie Lake in Princeton, N. J. My right middle finger remembers when I cut its tip off with a can of Spam in Panama. My left wrist remembers when I lifted a too-heavy piece of furniture when we were moving into a house at Kent Corners in Vermont.

My right wrist has a more unusual memory. At a ball in Helsinki in the 1930s, when it was permissible for gentlemen to kiss the back of the hand of a married lady whenever they met, or after a dance together, an amorous dancing partner, whose face I cannot now recall but my wrist remembers, turned my hand over at the end of a dance and tenderly kissed the inside of my wrist.

Of course my left little toe remembers when I broke it on the morning of our first day of visiting John in California. My throat remembers how terrified I used to be if anyone, teasingly, put their hands on my throat. (My throat suggests that I could find out why this is, if I liked.) And my left shoulder remembers those painful attacks of bursitis in New Hampshire.

I would like to be able to report that I still get these interesting messages when I do this exercise, but I don't. Perhaps, once my body gave the highlights of its experience it felt it didn't need to repeat it. Anyway, I can "sense" each part, I *feel* it, and it responds by tingling, but that is all. I am wondering if my concentration isn't as strong as it used to be, though I hope it's not that.

I think I should tell you that when I first did the exercises I discovered that I hadn't really known that my body was so neatly connected! It seems incredible but somehow I felt there were open spaces that separated parts of my body! Now, of course, I feel the connections strongly; I feel much more in touch with my body.

Although the effects of these exercises seem like magic—warming the hands, getting messages from our bodies—the Greens emphasize emphatically that this is not magic. They say bluntly, "Autogenic phrases are used not as magic formulas, but as a kind of map, a set of basic guidelines for the mind and the body."

You will find, as you learn to do whatever it is you want to do, you don't need to verbalize the process. Essentially, you are visualizing what you want done, giving your body an accurate picture of what you want it to do, and you will find it will do it.

I could go on quoting from *Beyond Biofeedback* indefinitely but I'll only give you one last word from the Greens: "After becoming conscious of body parts by traveling through the body, it is much easier to talk to the body for therapeutic purposes."

Later, I will describe to you the surprising results when I did this.

I am still re-reading *Beyond Biofeedback* and still learning from it, though I despair of understanding every concept in it. I made a note in my journal in 1990 that I can echo today:

June 20, 1990: I have been re-reading Beyond Biofeedback. *I have never read it carefully enough! I am learning a lot*

on this reading and even so I'm not getting it all. I guess I have
to grow some more.

SUMMING UP: I notice there are many doctors nowadays
who offer biofeedback to their patients. I have never gone
to one because I have never felt the need to. Elmer and
Alyce Green have given me enough ideas and information
to keep me busy for the rest of my life! And the book
doesn't use mechanical devices to measure skin tension
and blood pressure. You, of course, must make your own
choice in this area, but please try biofeedback, one way or
another.

CHAPTER ELEVEN

∅

Assagioli's
"Useless" Exercises

YOU MAY HAVE NOTICED that I have been going from
one source to another, trying to learn what I had to
do if I wanted to be in full charge of myself and, I
hoped, my life. Each of the kind, wise people I met up with
always passed me on to another ground-breaking pioneer
in the field of self-knowledge.

In Elmer and Alyce Green's book *Beyond Biofeedback*,
they spoke of Dr. Roberto Assagioli's ideas so compel-
lingly that I knew I must go to him next, so I wrote on
November 21, 1982, to my friendly bookstore, Kepler's in
Menlo Park, CA, asking for two books by Roberto
Assagioli, *Psychosynthesis* and *The Act of Will.*

It was Assagioli who gave me the quote from William
James that I then typed on a 3 x 5 card to tuck into the
blotter on my desk where I still see it every day. The
quotation was from William James' *Talks to Teachers* published in 1912. (So long ago and most people are still
unaware of its truth!)

The card is dog-eared and smudged but still clear:

"William James said: 'The man who has daily inured himself to the habits of *Concentrated Attention, Energetic Volition, and Self Denial in Unnecessary Things* will stand like a tower when everything rocks around him and his softer fellow-mortals are winnowed like chaff in the Blast.'"

I still thank Dr. Assagioli for this necessary reminder. It's very likely you've never heard of Roberto Assagioli. I hadn't either. He was born in Venice in 1888 and is considered to be in the top rank of modern psychologists along with Freud and Jung .

As soon as I began his book, *Psychosynthesis*, and discovered that he was saying that my body was not me, I said aloud, "Why, that's nonsense!" Of course my other "teachers" had implied something of the same thing and Gurdjieff made it quite clear with his metaphor of we, as drivers, trying to control our "troikas," but Assagioli was blunt. Not only my body wasn't me, neither was my mind nor my emotions. I simply couldn't believe it. It couldn't be.

I read on. I think what convinced me that my body wasn't me was his saying that when my body was tired, I was not tired. I realized, yes, being tired is only a physical thing and when I'm tired, I can lie down to rest my body and at the same time read a difficult book.

But my mind was not me? I thought of my mind as an instrument I tried to keep sharp and strong. I thought if my mind wasn't me, then I was nothing. If what I thought was not who I was, then I was nothing. But Assagioli wickedly pointed out that if I was reading a difficult book that I really wanted to grasp, my mind might suddenly tell me it was tired. It would refuse to read any more, and then of course I would have to give up. I was at once convinced. I had had that experience many times. (No need to describe to you my emotions which change and ebb and flow and flood; they have their own life, though I try to control them.)

So there you have Assagioli. Yes, but he was much more than that. He gave us exercises to train ourselves to believe our bodies are not us, and better still, to take advantage of this knowledge. His books explain these exercises. I put some on tape. I'm going to listen to the dis-identification, the "I am not my body" exercise right now.

℘

I'm back. That's such a wonderful tape, his language is so exact. I was smiling and laughing all through it. I'd like to quote it in full, but it would be better if you got hold of the book. (If you do, skip right to the exercises, the preliminaries are pretty technical.)

I got my Assagioli books at Christmas. I find that the first entry in my journal that refers to him was at the end of January, 1983. It was a long entry.

He says, "I have a body but I am not my body. I have an emotional life but I am not my emotions. I have an intellect but I am not that intellect. . . . All these instruments are changeable and impermanent, but can be dominated, disciplined, deliberately used by the 'I.' The 'I' is simple, unchangeable, constant and self-conscious."

This seems to be true. And this morning when I got up I began to follow this idea further. Because of medication, my body is tired and uncomfortable today. Because my body is heavy and doesn't want to take a brisk walk (and it's raining) I thought, "Damn! I'm tired before I start the day — and I hoped to work on my book this morning!" I felt sick and discouraged.

But why should I feel that way? Because it's a long-established habit to tie up mental work with how my body feels? Shouldn't I think of my body and my mind as separate? And also the emotions? Should I let myself indulge in depression because I can't—I imagine I can't—work on my book?

Why won't I accept that my body is tired and therefore decide not do a lot of typing? Why don't I do other work? I could do the physically easy, and also pleasant work, of working on my journals? And now my mood lifts!

The next month Fred had a sort of setback. I was so surprised and disappointed I simply couldn't get it out of my mind, so again I tried to follow Assagioli's advice.

February 15, 1983: I am upset. I keep telling myself, not only my body is not me, my emotions aren't either. I should visualize myself as strong, steady, unchanging, behind the tumult of my emotions. I don't have a clear image of myself, my essential self. I see myself as a mixture of my roles: wife, mother, friend, writer, etc. I guess I am saying that I only see myself as others picture me and they don't see the actual me at all. Don't even glimpse it. I'm going to work on visualizing the essential self that is hiding behind those roles and behind my emotions and "intellect." If I can grasp this concept, it might steady me, make me less vulnerable to how other people feel about me. I might even behave better!

You can see from that passage, that though I had been trying for years to become "inner-directed" rather than "outer-directed," which is of course what Assagioli is driving at, I had not been very successful, but I hadn't given up.

So I made that tape and, though I didn't follow Assagioli's advice to listen to it every day, I listened to it often. And I added to that his one on visualization. I worked hard on that particular tape, but perhaps because it involved numbers and I am a fool about numbers, I didn't do well at it. Finally, I went back to the visualization I told you about earlier, of changing colors. But I didn't give up on Assagioli. I began trying other exercises, some simple, some strange. I'll tell you about them. However, I must warn you that you will consider most of the exercises as "useless." So let me quote Dr. Assagioli, who himself calls the exercises "useless."

This is, of course, from *Psychosynthesis:* "The Performing of Useless Exercises: This technique is the performing of actions which have no utility whatever in themselves, and are performed for the sole purpose of training the will. They can be compared to muscular exercises in gymnastics which have no economic or other utility except the developing of the muscles and the enhancing of neuromuscular and physical well-being in general."

(There is something about Dr. Assagioli's language that appeals strongly to me. I hope you enjoy it too.)

If the good doctor's remarks about his exercises don't make you feel you want to try them, hear the opinion of Elmer Green in *Beyond Biofeedback:* "The profound effects of the exercise of volition have been recently emphasized by Roberto Assagioli, the creator of Psychosynthesis. Even making oneself stand on a chair for ten minutes is a simple exercise that can have far-reaching consequences."

The exercise Green mentions is a good example of an exercise that seems absurd. I will report to you later on my own experience with it. I did not begin with it, however. I first did the dis-identification, gave up on the visualization, and went on to one I knew I needed: The exercise "for evoking serenity." My life seemed so turbulent, I was scarcely able to handle it. I'll listen to that tape now.

ॐ

Well, that "Serenity" tape is amazing. I hadn't listened to it for quite a while and I had almost forgotten it. I was surprised that it had so many suggestions for useful ways to calm oneself. I'll quote the one I particularly liked: "Imagine yourself in circumstances that would tend to agitate or irritate you; for instance, being in the midst of an excited crowd—or in the presence of a hostile person—or confronted by a difficult problem—or obliged to do many things rapidly—or in danger— and *see* and *feel* yourself calm and serene."

That's a useful exercise, I think, but I remember another I like very much, too. Dr. Assagioli suggests that it is good ". . . to evoke serenity directly; try to *feel* it; with the help either of the repetition of the word or by reading some appropriate sentence, or by repeating many times a suggestive phrase or motto. For example: 'Both action and inaction may find room in thee; thy body agitated, thy mind tranquil, thy soul limpid as a mountain lake.'"

It's that quote that speaks to me. I can better imagine, hearing it, that my body, my mind and I myself are separate.

Dr. Assagioli didn't tell us where he found this line. I wish I knew who wrote it. Perhaps everyone knows it but me!

Patience was another quality that I needed very much at that time; I am a very impatient person, a slap-dash person, a gobble-my-dinner person. I still finish my dinner long before the others, but I am convinced that Dr. Assagioli or something else has given me the gift of more patience than I used to have. One of his exercises is directed solely at patience. I still have the little box I prepared for this exercise and I still have the small slips of paper I cut for it. The exercise was very simple. You make a small opening in a box and then, one by one, slip the pieces of paper into it. You are to do this slowly and calmly. I think I made one hundred pieces of paper so the process took some time. I did the exercise until I could do it without strain.

There was another exercise I did that I had to force myself into. It also was a simple one. I was to take a ruler and walk around my room, striking objects selected by me as I said aloud, "I *will* do this!" (That exercise is in *The Act of Will*.) I felt silly doing it and was glad that no one could hear me.

I have two accounts of the standing-on-a-chair-for-ten-minutes exercise. The first time I did it was March 1, 1983:

Thoughts while standing (for ten minutes) on a chair:

I felt perhaps I should be in a less personal room as I looked around this one. I am warmed by all the gifts I have been given: The African drum from Linda, the wooden stork from Sechil, Tim's painting on a rough board of a snail and a worm, the poster of an old woman from Doug, Oscia's card, "A clean house is the sign of a sick mind," etc. When I look around my room, I feel loved . (Perhaps this is actually good for me, because so often I have the feeling I am inadequate.) Then I thought my knees were beginning to feel weak and wobbly and my head achy and dizzy. But I remembered Assagioli's suggestion, "If you see yourself as ill, you will be ill." So I told myself firmly that I was well and would remain well. The ten minutes went by quickly.

The next report in my journal was in August, 1983. By then I had done the exercise several times and I think I recorded this one because I had enjoyed it so much.

I was doing Assagioli's standing-on-a-chair exercise. It's so great!

First I looked over at all my books and thought, not for the first time, that if I ever saw them in someone else's house, I would exclaim, "I'd like to have every one of them!" I'm so lucky to have them. I have only to look at the titles to remember what each one gave me when I read it for the first time—and the second.

I looked at the daguerreotype of Emily Rockwood in her teens and thought of her now at one hundred. And threw the ball right back at myself. Shall I live to be one hundred? If I do, I can't count on working between ninety and a hundred, but I should be able to plan on twelve more productive years as I am only seventy-eight as I write this.

And then I looked round at all my pictures of my friends and the beautiful fossil fish, and my friend from Istanbul, Betty Carp, smiling at me from the bookcase, and our snowy farmhouse above Adamant, Vermont, and the driftwood from the Roaring Branch in Arlington, Vermont, and I found I was grinning like a fool, completely happy.

I wonder now how Dr. Assagioli would have felt about these exercises to develop my will making me happy. Did that make them less effective?

Early in 1984, however, I began to have the unexpected feeling that perhaps I was developing strength. I put it down partly to Assagioli and all the other people who had given me advice, but also to an extraordinary experience that came my way. Unluckily, it is not one I can make available to you, but because it gave me such encouragement I feel it changed me. Thus, I must include it in this account of what brought me to where I am.

We had made friends with a talented artist who, if he made the effort, could see the colors in our auras that glowed invisibly for the rest of us. It was my good fortune that he volunteered to make a "portrait" of me, showing the colors that made up my aura. (I mentioned this earlier.) The "portrait" wasn't a likeness of me but of what I imagine he saw as my essence. Anyway, I gasped when he showed it to me, it was so beautiful.

The artist explained the significance of all the colors and ended by saying, "I imagine you know you are a healer." I hadn't known that! "You can certainly heal yourself and probably others, not only physically." This was a stunner.

I haven't quite finished with Dr. Assagioli. It's true I have stopped doing those exercises, partly because I'm so busy writing this book! But I think I will add the criticism I made of him in one of my last journal entries about him.

This was at the end of December, 1984, when I noticed a cartoon in the morning paper, which had Charley Brown taking Snoopy his dinner. Snoopy remarked, "I stay in close communication with my stomach," and I thought when I read it, that Dr. Assagioli would approve of that, which set me off thinking about his theories. I ended up writing in my journal:

I have come slowly to the conclusion that he is right and this has, among other things, made me more aware of my body. As a detached observer, I notice it more often and, for instance, question why it isn't feeling fine, instead of giving in to the not-feeling-fine mood.

I also seem to be able to be more detached about my emotions; they don't seem to have their same old power over me.

I wish I could say that now I have better control of my mind, but I still have to struggle to force it to read a difficult book, learn a list of words in a foreign language, or empty it of thought.

But there is one important subject that I must mention: Dr. Assagioli didn't mention that women must learn that they are not their husbands.

Perhaps I am the only one to have had such a delusion, but I have often found that I am tailoring my opinions to those of my husband, selecting clothes that will please him, cooking meals to his taste. Automatically.

I wonder if I can change this attitude after having been married so long; we were married in 1929.

SUMMING UP: Assagioli's own description of his "use-less" exercises is persuasive enough to make anyone want to try them: "They are for the sole purpose of training the will." Training the will is as important as meditation. They really go together. Try standing on that chair and let your mind go free. You'll find it a very refreshing exercise.

CHAPTER TWELVE

❧

Jaime Returns;
Other Unusual People
Turn Up

YOU MAY REMEMBER MY IMAGINARY DOCTOR, whom I summoned up when I was living in Vermont. If I didn't make it clear then, I should now, that I never could quite bring myself to believe that "he " was not just "me " speaking to myself. Any other view of him was, for me, incredible, although *The Well Body Book* unequivocally states that its authors believed such "apparitions" might be real.

I don't know how you feel about him, whether you consider him a wise man or a man of no substance, but in these later years, I have come to feel differently about him. Perhaps I have learned a little more. Elmer and Alyce Green certainly opened my eyes to unbelievable things that proved to be real. Whatever it was that changed my mind, I now feel that I don't really understand who Jaime is or where he comes from, but I'm sure he does not arise out of my imagination.

I had forgotten all about my Imaginary Doctor when I began to feel the need of help in California. If I had thought of him then, I would have consulted him. Instead I conjured up that beautiful little pet, the unicorn, but he proved not to be enough.

I think I'd have managed better if I hadn't kept remembering how the doctor had stressed the fragility of my husband's hold on life. He had improved a great deal after his stroke and was swimming three times a week, but I couldn't get out of my mind the doctor's remark, "Any morning you may wake up to find he has gone in the night!" This worked on me, not only emotionally, but physically and by the early 80s, my body began to express its tension by giving me a good deal of trouble with headaches, intestinal disorders, and sleeplessness. Then one night, my inner voice, Mary, asked me why I didn't get in touch with Jaime. I was ready to seize on any help I could get. The next day I meditated, and then through it journeyed back to Vermont to see if Jaime had forgotten me as I had forgotten him.

As I read over our conversation now, it seems such good advice that I feel I should read it over and over, just as I keep handy Gurdjieff's sensible, if difficult, suggestions.

I was nervous, almost as nervous as the first time I approached that white clapboard house in the woods in Vermont. Little had changed in the setting during my long absence, but there were spring flowers by the door this morning.

The journal picks it up:

When I opened the door of my room and went in, I looked across at the window. I could see the squirrel sitting on a long branch of the maple tree, his rich grey tail hanging down. He was staring intently at something on the ground. I couldn't see what it was, but anyway that was his business, not mine, so I wished him well and turned back to meet Jaime. As usual, he surprised me. I have a hard time not thinking he is simply an echo of my own ideas, but he again vividly proved he is himself, not me.

I didn't waste any time. I asked him right away, "What can I do to control my tension? All I can think of is to do relaxation exercises."

Jaime looked serious. "They are good but you must change your outlook. You must be happy."

I interrupted him: "How can I be happy when all my thoughts are unhappy?"

"You mustn't let yourself think unhappy thoughts; you must choose your thoughts!"

He isn't the first one to tell me that, I thought. But he was going on.

"You have a lot to be happy about. You have many friends. You should think happy thoughts when you go to bed—and when you wake up! Don't tell yourself you can't do as much as you used to. You're doing very well. You're doing fine!"

"But Fred looks so miserable! He gets so tired."

"He is here with you. Be happy about that. Be happy because he really loves you now."

I knew he was right. I looked at him. He was so big—so rough—so nice!

As he got up to go, I surprised myself by saying, "I'd like to hug you, Jaime. May I hug you?"

He smiled, a big smile.

"Sure, why not?" he said. He gave me an enormous bear hug. He smelled of corn, of tortillas and warmth.

"I love you, Jaime," I said.

"Yes. I love you. We love each other—in a nice way."

Then Jaime went back to Mexico.

I was still laughing at his final remark. Doctors are so cautious!

It was in 1985 when I had that conversation, and I spoke to Jaime several times after that, but it was in December, 1987, that I had another experience with Jaime that I must tell you about.

I traveled again back to Vermont, forgetting it would be winter there. The snow surprised me, deep and white. The bronze chrysanthemums by the door of the old house looked beautiful in their snowy caps. I kicked the snow off my shoes as I opened the door. Remembering our own old house in Vermont, I wondered if it would be cold inside, but warmth surrounded me as I went up the stairs.

When I looked out the window of my room, the squirrel wasn't there, but I saw the snow was crisscrossed with the tracks of small animals. I like California, but I wished then that I could put on my snowshoes once more. I wanted to investigate those tracks. I remember sighing as I turned back into the room. I sat down and called Jaime. I hoped he could help me with the headaches that were plaguing me.

When he came toward me, he took both my hands in his; my hands were swallowed up in his broad, strong, callused hands.

I don't know what possessed me but I blurted out, "Jaime, are you a doctor?"

"No. I wouldn't say so. Doctors usually prescribe medicine. I don't deal much in medicine." He smiled at me. "Yes, I know. You'd like to hear where I live and what I do for a living, that kind of thing. But that is temporal stuff. You already know the essential things about me, the important things, and that I'm happy when you call me."

So we talked about headaches. When we finished, Jaime really surprised me. He said, "I am going to give you a massage. Go over to that cot in the corner and lie down."

I have never had a massage. I even resist them. A friend had offered to give me one and had given one to Fred, but for some hidden reason, I hadn't wanted to try it.

But this morning I obediently lay down on the cot, face down, and Jaime massaged my neck and shoulders which had been hurting, and then he did my body and legs. I wondered if he would turn me over, but he didn't

When he was finished, he said, "Lie there for a few minutes. I'm leaving. Call me before you see the M.D. Please!"

"I will," I said. "Thank you very much. I feel much better."

And that was true. I found I felt relaxed all through my body, completely relaxed and comfortable. I still do.

You must remember that while all this was taking place, I was in my work room, sitting bolt upright in a straight chair. This is more puzzling to me, I think, than that Jaime comes when I need him. How can it be? That imaginary massage felt so good.

I will always be grateful to *The Well Body Book* for leading me to Jaime. I should also add that I have to be grateful to California, too, for when we got here I found a talented homeopathic doctor who, young though he was, always reminded me of an alchemist when he consulted his huge book of remedies. When he left this area, I was fortunate enough to find a Native American woman, an osteopath, who is the most sensitive, intuitive, caring physician I have ever encountered.

Anyway, I followed Jaime's advice. I kept thinking of my friends. I have such good friends, such warm and generous friends! And, of course, when I moved to California, it wasn't only Jaime and Mary I carried in my baggage, but also Aldous Huxley, Alan Watts and Gurdjieff.

In California I began to read about Buddhism. I read some of the usual authorities and then I found Janwillem van de Wetering.

I must tell you about him. The first book I discovered was *The Empty Mirror: Experiences in a Japanese Zen Monastery*, a vivid, humorous account of what working on Zen

Buddhism is really like. Van de Wetering followed this with another very readable book, *A Glimpse of Nothingness: Experiences in an American Zen Community.* Neither of these books made me want to join a Zen monastery, but I learned a great deal from them.

The Buddhists stress "non-attachment" and when I came upon that, I knew I could never be a good Buddhist. I am attached to too many things, too many people, too many pleasures. But I knew that I should at least attempt to work toward non-attachment, and I have, in varying degrees, ever since. One night in 1978 I dreamed of it.

Last night I dreamt that I was telling my son, John, and someone else that my friend, Mildred, who was somewhere between seventy and eighty, was busy and cheerful and writing a book. "She's happy, like me," I said, and started out of the room. I heard John laughing and turned back. "What's funny?" I asked.

"How can you say you're happy? That's really a joke!" He meant, I thought, that being old was so difficult, and, in addition, his father was ill, that no one old and with burdens could be really happy.

I said, "You have to have learned to do things for the pleasure of doing them, not for a reward, to give presents for the pleasure of giving, not for thanks. It's easy to be happy then."

I woke up thinking, "Yes, that would be non-attachment, and I haven't achieved it yet. That's why I cry when my sons misunderstand me and why I wish my grandchildren would thank me for my Christmas presents."

I'm a long way from non-attachment. I must work harder at it.

You, my reader, may also feel that non-attachment is beyond your grasp, but it's rather like meditation, even a little helps. As I write this, I'm sure I have gained a little of this desirable quality and what I have helps me take the bumps in the road almost lightly.

Of course, non-attachment is only a part of the teachings of Buddhism. I finally decided to copy out the main points made by van de Wetering, which I headed "READ AND RE-READ." I put it in my Day Book so I'd see it frequently. The advice is pretty simple.

"Buddhism is only specific about its methods. It tells you to meditate, to be conscious of what you are doing, to do your best. It doesn't like you to impose your opinion on others, and it stresses you should know yourself."

Not much new to you in that, is there? But if you're like me, you need to be told these things over and over again.

As you already know, it is not only Buddhism that has given me good advice. After we settled in California, I seemed to find one after another who gave me a lift. It made me think of myself as standing by the side of a highway, trying to thumb a ride, and someone always stops to take me further on my journey.

Dennis Jaffe is one. His book, *Healing from Within,* which has the appealing subtitle "How to Gain Greater Control over Your Own Health," supplied two very useful relaxation exercises.

Another book that encouraged me is called *Your Second Life,* by Gay Gaer Luce, which describes the amazing physical and mental things a group of older people were able to perform under her guidance. This would be a good book for you. One exercise in it is as mysterious as the Imaginary Doctor, though surely "The Healing Hand" must have some simple physical explanation. Anyway, it works!

The "Healing Hand" exercise will remind you of "Warming the Hands," but it involves concentrating on one hand, and is much more intense. It will actually soothe the pain in a sore muscle or a stiff neck and other simple strains. But I must emphasize that such exercises are not toys to play with. For instance, before applying the "Healing Hand," you must be sure that heat is the correct treatment for the injury or you may make things worse.

I must tell you about one more person who had some really encouraging ideas. He didn't furnish any exercises, nor was he explicitly interested in my—or your— growth, except in the most general way.

When I found A.H. Maslow's books, I was ready for them. Since World War II I had believed that wars were disastrous for the whole world, that not only the combatants suffered its effect, but all of us. I had also been convinced that the environmentalists were right: we were polluting the air we breathed and using up our natural resources at a deadly rate.

At the time I discovered Maslow, the loudest voices in the country were those who thought that nothing could be done to avert nuclear war except to be ready to strike first with our own bombs. The same people thought that it was only crazy environmentalists who foresaw disaster ahead if we didn't clean up the atmosphere, the land and the water.

It was wonderful to find there was a respected psychologist who believed people could be improved, that they could learn to live in harmony together. Maslow's voice didn't resound throughout the country, but more and more people were listening to him. He not only believed that there were ways to restore the equilibrium of the world, but that individually it was possible for a person to have a "peak experience" that changed his/her goals forever. I had never had a "peak experience"—at least I hadn't recognized it, if I had—but I found it encouraging to hear that such experiences were possible. Maslow also spoke of people who had developed to the point that they were able to live serenely and productively, making full use of all their creativity and abilities. He called such people Self-Actualized.

Here are a few of the qualities which Maslow felt distinguished these people from the crowd. He made clear that first one's basic needs must first be satisfied: shelter, security, acceptance and safety. Then one is free to develop the qualities he stresses:
Self-acceptance and acceptance of others
Spontaneity
Mystical or transcendental experiences
Democratic rather than authoritarian attitudes
Detachment from casual socializing
Involvement in a cause outside oneself
Autonomy

I have taken these attributes from a biography of Maslow, *The Right to be Human* by Edward Hoffman, an interesting account of Maslow's short life. He was born in 1918 and died in 1970.

All his life Maslow worked toward improving all of us, improving the world itself. Although he saw our culture clearly and often spoke of it as a "jungle," still he believed it was possible to change it. So I latched onto him. I read, marking many passages, his *The Farther Reaches of Human Nature* and then *Toward a Psychology of Being*. I was looking around for more of his writing when I discovered he had died.

Although Maslow didn't provide any "exercises" so far as I know, the qualities he stressed often develop, not from any specialized training, but from being aware, of knowing oneself and working to that end.

To finish up with Maslow, if you want to quickly and easily absorb a good many of his ideas, find Aldous Huxley's novel, *Island*, in your library. In Maslow's *Journal* he says "[I] re-read Huxley's *Island* ... & very much impressed. . . . Recommended it strongly to kids in motivation class."

I have only one *caveat* regarding Maslow. In my journal in 1986 I added an indignant note:

I am now further into Maslow's Journals, which show a side of him that isn't striking in his books. He downgrades women so incredibly that I am penciling outraged protests on almost every page. It's interesting that a person can be so brilliant, such a trail blazer, and have such a bias.

(I add today: I had forgotten this failing of Maslow's until I came upon this old journal. I love him anyway.)

So there you have Maslow. I hope that if you dip into his books, you will find them, as I did, stimulating, comforting, and amusing.

SUMMING UP: You should remember that even if you neglect for years a useful exercise, it will work if you try it again. Look at my faithful friend, Jaime!

You may be wondering what Buddhism has to do with growing older, but if you can accept that "non-attachment" is helpful, you will discover that possessions aren't as important as they were.

And, last, remember Maslow who allows you to feel optimistic about the future!

CHAPTER THIRTEEN

❧

Trying for a Miracle

AS WE HAVE BEEN GOING ALONG, talking about this and that, I hope you have been experimenting with relaxation exercises and visualization. Perhaps you have even begun doing them on a regular basis. You may be excited to have found out that you have more control of your body than before.

You may not want to go quite as far as I have, though it could be that just hearing something an ordinary person like me has been able to do may change your feelings about what is possible for you; it may give you a confidence you didn't have before. Let me tell you about it.

As you know, I had been reading many interesting books, several of them describing amazing developments in the control of the body by the mind. About this time (1990) I had picked up a book by Kenneth Pelletier, *Mind as Healer, Mind as Slayer: A Holistic Approach to Preventing Stress Disorders.* Having a friend who was going through a difficult time with cancer, I was struck by his account of Dr. Carl Simonton and his wife, Stephanie, who, while treating cancer patients, were combining traditional medicine with asking their patients to do intensive visualization at the same time. (Later, I got the Simontons' book, *Getting Well Again.*) I found their approach intensely interesting, although I couldn't know that I would be trying it myself before long.

But first I must go back in time and space to Salt Lake City, Utah, where, in the 1960s, my husband was teaching at the University of Utah. Salt Lake City is high, the air is clear, the sun is strong, and snow-capped mountains beckon from every horizon.

In those days no one I knew used a sunscreen. We didn't know we should protect ourselves from too much sun.

It was in Salt Lake City in 1964 that a doctor told me that the small lesion in the middle of my nose was skin cancer. He told me I had two choices, surgery or radiation. I thought radiation would leave a less noticeable scar, so I chose it. I didn't know, and I imagine many doctors didn't know then, that the use of radiation often results in a new cancer about twenty years later.

In Salt Lake in 1962 I had had a difficult time when I had been told I had a tumor on the back of my neck, which fortunately turned out to be benign. I had feared the worst, as my journal makes clear. (I must remind you that I didn't begin thinking about "work on myself" until we had left Salt Lake and settled in New Hampshire.)

February 7, 1964: I need to understand several recent things that have happened to me. The first is the skin cancer on my nose. There are a lot of things about that which puzzle me. My reaction, for instance. I didn't go into a tail spin, shaky, weepy, terrified, as I had two years earlier, but I did get shaky and scared over the visits to the doctors and the hospital. Even after I had learned it was not dangerous, I shook over the X-ray and the waiting room, especially seeing the wounded children.

And then we moved to California. In 1986 a dermatologist unexpectedly told me he had to do a biopsy on a small lesion on the left side of my nose, and soon afterward his lab told him they had found basal cancer cells in the specimen. It was then the doctor told me that having had radiation made it almost inevitable that cancer would recur. Now I must have surgery, he said, "Microscopic Controlled Excision," which would be done by a plastic surgeon. He would remove a minute slice of my nose, send it to the lab, while I waited "off-stage," and I would be called back to have another slice removed, wait again and again, until, at last, the specimen would show itself free of basal cells. I was warned that I must be prepared to be at the clinic all day.

On the day of the operation, the surgeon performed skillfully and delicately, especially the sewing up afterwards. My nose now looks as if a tiny sewing machine had placed about thirteen little stitches down it As I remember it now, I was only a little late for lunch, though I didn't feel like eating a great deal.

Okay. Now I must tell you that in May, 1990, the same dermatologist did a biopsy on the right side of my nose. When I returned to get the report the doctor, who by now was my friend, didn't look directly at me as he reported the biopsy had been positive. He went on, "I'm sorry to have to tell you that this time it's different, more serious. This time we found not only basal cells, but squamous. Squamous cells wander. You may have to have a skin graft."

I had never heard of squamous cells, though I was familiar enough with basals. I was thinking that squamous sounded horrid, when I noticed that the doctor had dropped his voice, as if he was talking to himself. He was muttering the word *disfigurement*. I didn't like the sound of that, but driving back home, I kept telling myself I had handled this before, I could handle it again. But to go through that unpleasant ordeal, and then the days of dressing the deep wound at home—oh, I didn't want to go through that again!

Two days later I met the surgeon, a different man, but very pleasant. He made our meeting almost a social affair as he reminded me that my son, Douglas, was also his patient. (Doug is a long-distance runner, exposed to the sun for long periods of time.)

The doctor was smiling and he used a delightful expression when he spoke of Doug. "I know now where he gets his salt and vinegar; you both are independent people!" He then reminded me that I must be ready to spend the entire day at the clinic. "The nurse will give you the date for the operation."

It was a nice nurse whom I'd gotten to know during the first operation, but I was stunned when she told me that the first date free for the operation was six weeks hence.

Six weeks! On the way home I thought that waiting six weeks was almost as big a hurdle as the operation itself. Six weeks! A month and a half. Forty-two days! Before I reached home, I had decided to try to use the time. I remembered that book by Kenneth Pelletier in which he spoke of Dr. Carl Simonton's method of working with cancer patients, all of whom had very dangerous, life-threatening cancers. Mine, of course, was only a little cancer.

Once home, I ran out to my workroom and began pulling books from the shelves. What luck! On page 255 of Pelletier's *Mind as Healer, Mind as Slayer,* I found just what I needed: "For the treatment the patients are instructed to relax deeply three times a day, while mentally picturing the destruction of material by the body's immunological system and disposal of it through the circulatory system takes place."

I was wondering how I could do this when I remembered my friends, Elmer and Alyce Green. In *Beyond Biofeedback* they had described the method of Jack Schwartz, a powerful psychic, for healing a wound in his hand. I found the passage. There it was, perfectly clear: "First practice some autogenic exercises for quieting the body and the emotions." And then he thought of his hand becoming large as a house, and *he went inside his hand and repaired it!*

The next morning (May 26, 1990) I hung a sign for Fred on the door of my work room, PLEASE DON'T KNOCK! First I did my regular relaxation exercises and then I lay on my couch (my grandmother's couch—surely that helped!) I began to think about my problem. I pictured the squamous cells in my mind; they showed up as black, scaly, whiskery creatures, rather like deformed lobsters. The basals were simpler, plain blue-black beetles. I knew I needed someone to help me and I thought of the white cells in my blood that fight disease.

I was fully relaxed when I went over to sit in my meditation chair. My eyes wide open, I began by counting my breath as it came in, ten times, and then as it went out, ten times. Finally I counted my breath going in and out twenty times. By then my eyes were out of focus and I saw that the inside of my nose was open before me, and I went in. I left the gigantic me behind sitting in that hard chair as, like Alice in Wonderland, I became the right size to walk around inside my nose.

To my surprise, I was in a beautiful white cavern, its walls and floor smooth as alabaster but giving out a faintly rosy glow. At the back I noticed a tunnel leading up and out of the cavern, and off to my left, I saw an open canal about two feet long and perhaps a foot wide; streaming through it was a bright red torrent. Somehow I knew this was my blood stream.

I heard a slight sound and, coming down the steep incline, out of the tunnel, was a file of some six or eight small men-like creatures in white suits, white caps, shoes and gloves, white surgeon masks across their faces. They were carrying silver spears. They were my white corpuscles! I had stepped into another world, crossed a border, landed on the moon! But, though the setting was bizarre, it seemed perfectly natural.

I spoke silently to the men in white, as if in my head, and I heard their answer in the same way.

I said, "Welcome! You've come to help me, haven't you?"

The leader answered, "Yes, we were called."

I described to them the nasty black squamous cells and the blue-black basals and explained their destructive function.

The leader looked at me solemnly over his surgical mask. "We are healers. It is not for us to kill things. But I can see these are dangerous entities and should be killed."

We were both rather formal. I said, "It's easy to spot them, isn't it? Those dark splotchy ones among the healthy cells must be them."

"We see them," he answered, and they got to work, spearing the enemy one by one, depositing them in the blood stream as it raced by.

After I had watched them work a while, I asked, "Will it be okay to meet twice a day?" (Simonton had suggested three times a day, but I knew that was impossible for me.)

"We can do that. Just call us and we'll come. It's like a holiday for us, doing this different work."

I found I was feeling tired. "Good, thank you! I'll see you this afternoon then," and I came back to the room and myself, relieved and happy. I didn't know whether my friends and I could make any difference, but it was a relief to be doing something, not just waiting for the surgeon's knife.

That night I called Jaime. It was beautiful in Vermont, green, spring flowers in the woods.

May 27, 1990: I saw his shoes, dusty as usual, his blue jeans, not new, and then there was Jaime. He came toward me. He didn't seem quite real and I told him so. He said, "Take my hand!" It was reassuringly hard, calloused.

"Yes, you're real now," I said. I explained my visualization.

Jaime smiled. "Let's think about it. Yes, your white soldiers can kill this enemy. They're killable—even doctors know that! They don't have to be cut out, if you can kill them inside. What you must do is to make it perfectly clear what you want the white soldiers to do and you must have an exact idea of how you see the white warriors and the forms of the squamous and basal cells."

"Yes, I've done that."

I felt better after I'd talked with Jaime. He was so encouraging and explicit. Dr. Simonton felt that this method would not be successful if the patient didn't have the full support of his family. I had not only my family behind me, ("If anyone can do it, you can!") but I also had the advice of Jaime, who straddled both my worlds. And we still had five-and-a-half weeks. July 6 was the date.

Of course I kept a detailed account of our activities in my journal. The journal makes entertaining reading because I kept on with my usual routine. I was still a "loner," I didn't want anyone to know who might have scoffed at what I was trying to do, so in between the accounts of the visualization—*This performance is taking on a life of its own!*—would be tea parties, the Sunday Peace Vigil that Fred and I were running, and doing the laundry. Sometimes our tea parties lasted so long that I would have to ask Fred if we could go out to dinner because there just wasn't time enough to cook dinner and do the visualization. I remember once, while I was serving tea and we all were talking about politics, I wondered how my friends would react if I suddenly told them that that morning I had been inside my nose. It had been an unusual experience that day because the leader of the "white army" had suggested that we check out the left nostril that had been operated on four years earlier. He wanted to be sure there were no malignant cells lurking in there. So we had all trooped up the tunnel in the right side and then turned to go down the left side. Going down that passageway was difficult, as the earlier operation had twisted it and the footing was uneven. We found nothing but I think one of the soldiers checked it out every week just to be sure.

On June 14, the journal reported:

My White Army has come up with a new idea: to get the normal cells to squeeze out the abnormal squamous and basal cells and when they are squeezed out, the warriors will kill them, They have explained to the healthy cells that if they can get rid of the bad cells, the doctor's scalpel won't come among them cutting and cutting. They, the healthy cells, are being very cooperative!

There is a long entry for June 26:

I wish I were more confident about the "work" I am doing with my White Army. When I'm doing it, I feel it's for real, that they are really finding and killing the squamous and basal cells. But when I leave my room and enter the everyday world, I am not sure.

I get into this scene by beginning to meditate and counting my breath in three different ways. Almost always when I finish the third, I can enter my nose, though occasionally I can't make it! I hear my friends saying, "You aren't clear yet! Come out of the clouds!" and I do.

The whole thing is an amazing experience. We have eight more days to work. The leader said today, "We don't know how many bad cells there are, do we? And so we won't know if we've gotten them all." And then he added. "But if, at the end of the operation, the surgeon says, 'It wasn't as bad as I had expected!' that will be good enough for us," And it certainly will be good enough for me!

I had begun to worry about the operation. My journal of July 5, 1990:

I looked up the experience of four years ago. It took me a week "to be on deck again," but this year I'll have to manage better. Fred is too frail, too easily tired these days to be able to handle the housework for a week. I hope the operation goes better, too. I had "terrible headaches." Maybe I won't this time. I hope!

And then my journal's account of the operation.

The nurse, Jo Ann, came for me, tucking my hand under her arm. We had to wait a long time in the operating room. Jo Ann kept chatting. A young woman doctor and a student appeared. The woman pumped the anesthetic into my nose, doing it so slowly and gently it didn't hurt at all. I asked Jo Ann to tell Fred because he knew that had been the only part I dreaded.

The surgeon came. They taped down my eyes. He worked away, Then Jo Ann said, "You'll hear some buzzing," which I did and there was a smell too, my flesh being cauterized. Then I was able to see again and Jo Ann took me to the waiting room.

I think I waited nearly an hour before Jo Ann came to take me back for another slice, but as we walked to the operating room together, she said, "We're only going to put a Bandaid on your nose and you can leave. There was nothing to be found! The result was negative!"

I stopped short. I couldn't believe it. "Wow!" I said and then I told Jo Ann what I had been doing. She knew about Dr. Simonton's work and I could see she was not skeptical. She asked me how long I had been doing the autogenic exercises. "About ten or twelve years." As the doctors came in, I said, "Shall I tell them?"

"You must tell them!" So I did. The surgeon smiled cheerfully, but didn't laugh or put me down. "You'll heal perfectly,"

he said. "Change the dressing just as you did the other time, and there will be no sign of the operation in a few weeks."

Once home, I summoned my victorious white army and all of us danced for joy. I still had to change the dressing on the wound twice a day, which was a nuisance, involving peroxide, an antibiotic salve and a new Band-aid. It then occurred to me that my little friends could easily heal the wound overnight. I was thinking about this when I heard an impersonal voice, "You don't realize how much energy your body had to put out in order to kill those cells. Don't ask anything more of it for a while."

Then I remembered reading in *Beyond Biofeedback* that Jack Schwartz took time to ask his body if was okay before he thrust the steel needle through his arm for the second time. I let my small wound heal itself.

When I returned to the dermatologist for him to check the healing, he told me he had been sent the clinic's laboratory report. He read it to me. It was quite technical but it stated clearly that only two basal cells had been found—and of course the surgeon's knife had disposed of them.

The dermatologist looked puzzled. "I saw those squamous cells with my own eyes," he said, shaking his head. I don't know how he explained it to himself; perhaps he decided that the lab had mixed up samples.

So there it is. The right side of my nose has no tiny stitches in it and I was spared a lot of pain.

Have I made the experience sound easy? It was not. It took self-discipline and deep concentration. Doing it twice a day wasn't easy either. There seemed to be so many valid reasons to skip a session. It was difficult to center down, to maintain the deep concentration needed to keep me inside that nose.

I remember my son, the long-distance runner. For years he ran the Western States Endurance Run, a 100-

mile race on mountain trails from Squaw Valley, California, up over the mountains to the canyons of the American River and on to Auburn. To be able to do this, Doug trained year-round.

If I hadn't done those autogenic exercises all those years and if I hadn't practiced visualization as a writer, I do not believe I could have brought this effort to a successful conclusion.

SUMMING UP: I hope that none of my readers who has been trying to follow the path to a cheerful old age will have cause to apply under such unpleasant pressure the skills and self-discipline you have learned along the way. But if you should have to, I can tell you that you will be very glad to be able to do something to help your body recover from such a threat.

CHAPTER FOURTEEN

≴

Where I Am Today

NOW WE ARE IN THE '90s, and, though I don't know how old I'll be by the time you are reading this, at the moment it is February, 1994, it is raining, and I am sitting here thinking about being eighty-eight.

At this point you are probably asking for a report on where all this "work on myself" has brought me, so this chapter will be "Rebecca as an Old Woman," though you may remember that my cousin, Emily Rockwood, told us we aren't old until we are ninety which, I hope, gives me time enough to finish this book. (If I'm lucky, I may even see it published.)

First I must tell you that a month after that non-operation on my nose, my husband had another stroke. This time he was robbed of the ability to read, which was tragic as he had been translating the autobiography of a Turkish statesman. It was a 200-page book and Fred had only fifteen pages to go before he completed the job. Those fifteen pages are still untranslated.

Do you remember that I had managed to set aside Tuesdays in which to work all day? I had finished my

Foreign Service book and was beginning to look for a publisher. I dropped all that, of course. My husband wasn't paralyzed but he was very weak and confused. I took care of him, a full-time job. August 4, 1990, was the day I'll never forget.

I didn't write in my journal until August 22. I'm going to quote that first entry, though it isn't really relevant to the subject of this book, that is, to the path I had been trying to follow. I must correct that: *the path I am trying to follow.*

August 11, 1990, 5:30 AM So there it is. I just dreamed that I drove Fred and me over a cliff, asking as I did it, "Why have I done this? Well, good-bye, Fred," I said as the ground rushed up to meet us.

For not only Fred's life as he knew it has ground to a halt, but my life has come to a stop, too. No more trying to do serious writing, no more trying to send out stories to editors, no more Tuesdays alone in my workroom!

For it's not only that Fred can't stand having me out of his sight but also that real communication with him is over, at least for now, if not forever.

There! I hear him in his bathroom. He will want his breakfast if he notices, through the crack in my door, that the light is on in my room. 5:45. I thought I had at least fifteen minutes more to myself!

Anyway, I vow I'm going back to writing in this journal and us soon as Fred can let me, I'm going to spend an hour a day in that room of mine. I can do "busy" work like an inventory of my files.

But I must watch that I don't get too tired to do all the housekeeping, errands and my own work. I must be more efficient, more disciplined, if I can.

It may amuse you to know that all through this I hung on to Dr. Assagioli and during the flood of phone calls asking how Fred was, when the caller asked how I was, I always answered, "My body is exhausted, but I'm fine."

I'm not going to inflict the whole sad story on you, but I will tell you that from time to time I remembered Vermont, realizing that, though this situation was much more serious, I was handling it better. This house in California doesn't have two floors, but I knew then that if it had offered me the chance to step off at the top of a flight of stairs, I wouldn't have taken it. Nor did I have another suicidal dream.

I feel, of course, that it was the "work" I had been doing that had given me the strength, patience and self-discipline I needed.

I made my state of mind explicit in a journal entry dated August 23, 1991, just a little over a year after Fred had become incapacitated. I couldn't believe what I knew to be true, but this was probably the reason I finally told myself that I could no longer ignore my own needs. My role as nurse-attendant-cook-chauffeur, etc. had blotted out the writer-reader-student. I saw I was as cloistered as a nun.

August 23, 1991: How can I be happy? Fred is so frail! He fell asleep on the sofa at tea; he snored! Earlier I had watched him swim; it hardly seemed worth his effort. He very slowly swam the length of the pool, twice, I think, and then sat in the Jacuzzi for perhaps five minutes and then, slowly, climbed out and began, slowly, to dress. It was this exertion that had tired him so.

How can I be happy? Our future is so uncertain.

How can I be happy? I am always tired.

How can I be happy? I lie awake at night, unable to sleep.

How can I be happy? My time for writing is so fragmented, I can't even manage to send out pieces I wrote a while back, and if I think of a new one I want to do, there is no time.

How can I be happy?

Yet deep inside, I am happy. Deep inside something, some-one, is singing. Why? Even my body seems receptive to happi-ness; my mouth breaks into a smile when there is nothing to smile about.

But there it is. I am happy, even if it doesn't show, even if it goes against all reason, even though I will shortly be eighty-six.

I took my first step back to my own life a little later. I had given Fred his lunch and he had gone off to take a long nap which freed me to go out to lunch with Lois, a good friend. We went to a local Chinese restaurant where my fortune cookie gave me the message, "Your mind is filled with new ideas. Make use of them." That night I made an entry in my journal:

January 28, 1992: I am not sure I came to this decision at lunch or after Lois had left for Half Moon Bay, but she so invigorated me that it's probably why I have decided again to take Tuesday mornings to work. Being away from Fred for four hours in one day shouldn't be too much of a strain on him. It shouldn't make me too tired to be able to do the housework the rest of the day.

Taking Tuesday mornings, however, didn't prove to be as practical as I had hoped. I felt frustrated because I couldn't get back to work in the afternoon; I found typing several hours tired me more than I had expected; and I soon realized I was cutting too many corners in my house-keeping duties.

It was then that I came upon that unexpected small ad in the magazine, *Poets and Writers*. It had been inserted by the Thanks Be to Grandmother Winifred Foundation that I told you about as I began this story.

I think you can understand that their award meant a good deal more to me than just that I would be free to work four mornings a week. In a subtle way, it validated my effort, made it seem a worthy project, and one that might make a real contribution. I still feel incredulous when I think about it.

Now we'll get back to how I'm doing. Let's take awareness.

Am I aware all the time, most of the time, or rarely? Certainly I am not aware most of the time, but I've developed the habit of telling myself, "Watch it! Be aware!" and then I try to see everything around me. I try to be aware of myself, how I am feeling, even how my muscles feel. I try to observe everything in detail.

How often do I do this? It hurts me to be honest, but let me tell you that as I write this, it is now after lunch, the middle of the afternoon, and I haven't yet told myself even once to be aware. Yesterday I probably did it twice. Oddly enough, I seem to be able to "wake up" most often when I am driving off alone on some errand, to the post office or the grocer. I am never "aware" when friends come to tea. (I must try this; it might be interesting.)

Once I was given a simple lesson. I'll tell you about it. (I found it in my journal):

I was walking down Gehricke Road under the tall eucalyptus trees, past the hillside where I often see a pair of long-eared California rabbits who live in a brambly patch of shrubs. I realized that for some minutes I had been lost to where I was, but knowing that, even when I was unconscious of my surroundings, my eyes were seeing everything. I told my eyes if they saw something I should see, please alert me. It wasn't until then that I saw lying on the road right in front of me, a broad, shiny black feather, a full foot long, gleaming in the sun like polished ebony.

I brought it home, of course. I put it up in this workroom where I am writing. I told my friend Michael about it. He was excited. "Did you know that Joseph Campbell said that feathers are considered by the Indians as carriers and communicators of spiritual power?"

So my feather was important to the Native Americans—and to me. Even so, that lesson, showing me so clearly what I may miss if I am not aware, hasn't cured me of thinking I am wide awake when in reality I'm fast asleep. I'm still a dilettante.

You'll want to know how I am doing on meditation, too. I have to tell you my meditation these days is set forth in this journal entry:

May 17, 1990: I have been re-reading my Zen books when I'm in bed at night. Philip Kapleau, and Suzuki's "Essentials of Zen Buddhism," and I'm enjoying again Janwillem van de Wetering's experiences.

This has spurred me into trying harder to find time every day to meditate for ten minutes. I don't know why I resist so stubbornly. I usually tell myself there isn't time, or I must work on the inventory of my files, or write in this journal. Yet I never miss the twenty-minute meditation I put on my schedule for Tuesdays, my work day. Is that simply because I enjoy putting check marks by the tasks I have set myself? I'm so simple-minded that I've probably hit on the reason.

I haven't improved to a noticeable degree since I wrote that, though I have now progressed to fifteen minutes a day. Luckily, as I have told you before, meditation works even if you aren't very good at it. Nowadays I am always hoping that the fifteen minutes will improve my concentration, as that seems to float out of my reach just as I am grabbing for it.

Have I ever told you that, although I know for a fact that getting old is a fast and irreversible process, I have never quite believed this is true? I keep thinking that, though I can't walk as far this year as last, next year I'll do better!

It's part and parcel of this attitude that made me confess to my friend, Cynthia, when she asked me the question directly, "Rebecca, how old do you actually feel?" I had to answer, "Cynthia, it's silly, I know, but when I think of my age, I'm in my seventies, not late eighties!"

I remember that once, some years ago, my then-young but astute grandson asked me a surprising question, "Grandma, do you know your hair is white?"

I laughed, but if I had been honest I would have told him I often forgot it. Sometimes I am startled when I catch sight of myself in a mirror.

Probably that's why I wish people would forget my age. My journal explains it:

April 24, 1993: I've gotten so cocky that I forget I am old and wrinkled, that I must walk slowly, watching where I go because I'm afraid of falling.

Speaking of falling, all my friends have suggested I use a cane, but I know, though I haven't said it aloud, that the reason I won't consider a cane is because I feel myself to be straight, tall, strong and healthy, not a stooped old woman of eighty-seven.

And yet, I have to admit, I have acquired one of the accepted failings of getting older: I forget things. I have to make lists, and often when I go to the grocer's with a long list, I find when I come home I've forgotten to get something highly visible on that list.

But once in a while I remember something I thought I'd never drag up out of the depths of—what? My subconscious? The incident I am about to tell you was surely a gift from one of my "other selves," not from the everyday me.

We had gone down to stay overnight with our son, John, who lives a hundred miles from us, in the mountains. Because young people are naturally warmer than old people, I packed my warmest clothes, including a flannel nightgown and warm bedroom slippers, that I don't need at home.

Later, when I unpacked after our visit, I couldn't find my little traveling clock. My brother had given it to me and I used it to wake me for my glaucoma eye drops. I couldn't find it anywhere, so I called John.

John, like most people, has one of those walk-about-phones, so as we were talking he went into the guest room. "It's not on the bureau, Mom!" Then, "Not on the night table, Mom!" and finally, "Not under the bed."

That night I had to use the strident alarm clock that I had long ago abandoned.

The next morning I was doing a relaxation exercise. I have found that then, my mind, released from any special duties, often has unusual ideas. This time, to my surprise, I unexpectedly saw myself standing in John's guest room. Actually, I was standing behind myself, watching me pack my suitcase. Then I saw that I had the little clock in my right hand and I was tucking it into the toe of my warm slipper.

When the exercise was finished, I went at once to my clothes closet. There on the floor, inside the warm slipper was the little clock. (I think I would have been more surprised if it hadn't been there.)

(But I am no Miracle Woman. At this very moment I am looking for a journal entry I want to copy for you, but I can't find it!)

Another aspect of my getting old is the way I feel about people. I remember reading a review of an autobiography of a well-known woman writer. The reviewer reported that the writer had found, as she moved into her seventies, that she rarely met people who interested her—people she would like to know better.

I am not a well-known writer. I live a quiet life, not meeting many people, but my experience has been just the opposite. I find that almost everyone I meet is, not only likable, but frequently lovable. If it didn't sound so foolish, I would be tempted to say that, instead of criticizing, even despising, a good many people as I did when I was young, I love a great many people. (Should I add, as Jaime did when we hugged each other, "We love each other *in a nice way*"?)

I think I can truthfully say that I have never had so many friends. They are not only interesting and stimulating; they are generous and uncritical. Most of them are women, though there are four men on the list.

I don't know how to describe how these friends make me feel. They keep in touch—many are not in California and one of my closest friends lives in Ankara, Turkey—and when I need help of any kind, they are ready. I never imagined that anyone could be so supported, so enveloped in this wonderful feeling, knowing friends are available at any time for anything: a trip to the emergency room, an errand in the next town, or just coming to tea on a rainy day. I am blessed!

The other day I went to a stationery store in town. I was buying some notebooks for my journals and when I was offered a dozen, I laughed. "I'd really like to take twelve," I said, "but I feel I'd be challenging fate. I can't be sure, at eighty-eight, that I'll be here long enough to fill a dozen notebooks."

The saleswoman looked at me thoughtfully. "Someone must be caring for you," she said.

I was surprised. "Why do you say that?"

"Someone *must* be looking after you! I would never have thought you were eighty-eight!" Of course, it is not a person who is looking after me; it's the path I am on.

By now you must have a good idea of how I am now that I am reaching the end of the long road that I chose in Antrim, New Hampshire, in 1968. It must be clear to you that, though I have an ordinary mind and started out with very little self-discipline and even less understanding the powers we all have, I have been gradually led to this happy place where I can handle my problems and enjoy my old age.

Of course I haven't forgotten those friends who guided me, urged me on, lent me the benefit of their experiences. I still try to follow Gurdjieff's advice to do one difficult thing every day—I often don't have to look for it, it presents itself, like the income tax forms — and to break a habit, any habit. Every day I do exercises given me by Mike Samuels, Dennis Jaffe and Elmer and Alyce Green. I am always quoting Dr. Assagioli, and Alan Watts. As for Jaime and Mary, I still consult them regularly. Jaime is still telling me unpleasant truths I should have recognized by myself. Mary is just as severe about my writing style. So nothing much has changed really.

SUMMING UP: It's true nothing has changed very much, yet everything has changed if we go back to that little redwood house in the woods in Antrim, New Hampshire. When I remember how confused, how insecure, how lost I felt then, I have to admit that to have left all that behind me is a miracle. I am a very lucky woman.

CHAPTER FIFTEEN

℘

Make Your Body
Your Ally

I T WAS IN TURKEY AND I WAS SIXTY-ONE when I discovered
for the first time that my body no longer was able to
obey my every command.

We were leaving after visiting two Peace Corps volun-
teers who were working in a small Turkish village. Our
friends had just flagged down a bus to take us to the
railroad station in the nearest town. As the bus came to an
impatient stop, I said good-bye, and then found I couldn't
make it up the high step into the bus. I had to be ignomini-
ously boosted by a friend.

I have not forgotten my embarrassment, nor have I
forgotten the village of Bereketli, for we had had a rare
experience the night before: dinner at the home of the
muhtar, the mayor. I must share it with you.

We had left our shoes by the door as we entered the
little stone and adobe house and were greeted by the
smiling mayor, who settled us down on cushions around
a low table in a corner of the small room. Three children

were spread-eagled asleep in a corner, the only light a lantern hung on a nail on the wall beside us. Slightly swaying above our heads was a sleeping baby in a wooden cradle suspended from the low ceiling.

The *muhtar's* wife, too shy to sit with us, came to set in the center of the table a small dish holding about a dozen green beans covered with yogurt, garnished with fresh garlic. We helped ourselves, carefully, (there were six of us) with a wooden spoon. The next course was eggs, probably three, scrambled in oil in a small pan; they were decorated with paprika. Then the dessert, a tiny, airy semolina pudding baked with cheese.

There had been an unexpected guest, an old man who wanted to talk about Ataturk, his hero, with the visiting history professor (Fred). In patched clothing, he had wound a woolen scarf high around his cap in nostalgic imitation of the outlawed turban. As he sat down, his tall turban-cap set the baby's cradle swinging.

Ahmet Efendi soon made it clear that we were present at a feast for I, thinking to be polite, had asked the *muhtar* the age of the baby above us when the old gentleman turned, saying sharply to me, "Don't talk, Lady, *eat, eat!*"

I have never forgotten that hospitable, friendly, poverty-stricken village where nobody was overweight, but I have to confess I did let myself forget for a while that I couldn't get on that bus without help, until my body reminded me in much the same humiliating way.

But now I must return to our subject, our bodies. First of all, I can tell you that you'll find out that, like meditation, your body will forgive a lot. You may not have thought about it at all until it failed you in some way or, if you have been lucky, you have never had such a reminder.

From my perspective, most of you have magnificent bodies, but you often abuse them. I don't mean with drugs or alcohol, I mean by not giving yourself enough sleep, relaxation, or even food. You often do this for no very good reason. You have assumed your body is your slave, and your body hasn't begun to talk back—yet. But it will!

You may still be getting up in the morning with that wonderful feeling of well-being, sure the world is your nut to be cracked open, that the space above and around you is infinite, waiting to be explored. You can indulge yourself in the delights of skin-diving, of lying on the sand in the warm sun, of driving a car up a twisting, winding coast road, running across the beach to enjoy intense pleasure of diving into the surf. I myself used to enjoy putting my horse into a gallop across a meadow, and I loved to whirl around in a fast polka to gypsy violins.

It's different now, of course. Perhaps you, too, may have had hints that your body isn't as responsive as it used to be.

I suggest that from now on you think of your body as your friend, your ally. I switched to this viewpoint in my sixties when I began to think of the years ahead. I learned then that my body and I could have a new relationship. We began to be partners in the effort to live to a pleasant old age. I don't mean to suggest that I have stopped wishing I could jump on a spirited horse or find a partner for a polka; that's like smoking. (Even though I stopped smoking many years ago, there are still times when I'd l love to smoke a cigarette!) but I realize that I have out-grown such pleasures.

We must not forget, however, that even when we aren't young, our bodies still enjoy being exercised; it's only that the exercise takes less energetic forms. Probably when you were young, you didn't think of "exercise." Who thinks of tennis or swimming as "exercise" when it is just fun to be doing something with your friends? But when you are older, you should program your exercise.

I was thinking about this in 1972, writing in my journal:

I think it is true, generally, that many people don't enjoy the physical use of their bodies after, say, fifty, except in bed, and that's a different sort of exercise and a different sort of reward. But even at sixty-six, if I walk freely down the road beside the river, I feel more alive. If I climb up a hill and stand, puffing, at the top, I feel years younger. The play of muscle, the rush of blood through the body, the awareness—it's a good feeling!

I am paying now for never having been an athlete. The only "sport" I enjoyed when I was young was riding. I rode wherever I could, but when I married into the Foreign Service, I found little opportunity to ride. I remember in El Salvador I occasionally rode a mule to explore a friend's *finca*, and there is a yellowed snapshot of a little donkey carrying me up to the rim of a volcano. In Estonia I was very lucky; I was asked if I would like to exercise a beautiful Arabian stallion; the Estonian businessman who owned him hadn't time for riding. Then I had no riding for ten years, but in Tegucigalpa, Honduras, we were able to live a country life. I rode to market on horseback, the sun shining on the red head of my small son, Doug, bobbing alongside me on his pony. That sums up my exercise.

In your old age you may be able to participate in much more active exercise than I, since I have not had the long training of useful muscles that many of you may have had. You may arrive at your older years prepared to make sure you remain physically active.

When we arrived in California, because I didn't have an active sport to fall back on, I settled for walking regularly. I would have preferred to run; my favorite fantasy has always been that I'm running swiftly, lightly, stretching out, hardly touching the ground, the breeze on my face, the sun warm on the back of my head. I'm not even breathing hard. I am almost flying!

Realizing that fantasy was not for me, and spurred on by the gift by our son, Douglas, of a pedometer on our 50th wedding anniversary, I settled into walking, though I managed to be an active spectator when Doug began his annual competition in the Western States Endurance Run.

The Western States was a revelation. More than two or three hundred runners began the race every year at 5 AM at Squaw Valley, climbing up over Emigrant Pass and then down into the blazing hot canyons of the American River, hoping to finish the 100-mile course in at least twenty-four hours. The winners, of course, came in a good deal faster than that, though some others didn't wearily cross the finish line until dawn was about to break, and most didn't finish at all. My husband and I were members of Doug's family support crew for more than ten years, long enough to see that women not only were running along with the men, but eventually even finishing in the top ten.

One of the most amazing runners was Helen Klein who, in her sixties, was making and breaking world age records. She regularly completed the 100 miles of the Western States. I remember that in 1989 she broke her existing record in the 65-to-69 age group for 100 km. by twenty minutes! Another competitor who was a legend in San Francisco was Walt Stack. He was in his seventies when he completed the 100-mile Western States course, which not only asks the runners to climb mountains and endure the blistering summer heat of the canyons, but to ford the American River before they reach their goal in Auburn. Stack made it sound very simple in an interview, "It's just a matter of putting one foot in front of the other. Don't worry about breathing. Let the air come in any orifice it wants." And he added, "I know of one 72-year-old woman who decided to run marathons and spent the first four years walking. Then she began building up and she ran four marathons last year."

I am telling you this in order to encourage you to continue with whatever exercise you enjoy. If you are an ace at tennis right now, you probably can be an ace in your old age.

You may think, as I used to, that your muscles weaken with the years. They do, but not nearly as much from age as from not being used. Even if you have let them go until they are flabby and weak, you can bring them back with determination and self-discipline by using them. I can testify to this myself. Time and again something has kept me from walking—the flu, a busy schedule or incredibly bad weather—but now I know that, disagreeable as it is to force lazy muscles back into action, they can be subdued into doing their duty.

That isn't to say that everybody can be a world-class runner, swimmer or skier if they are starting from scratch. You can improve, you can become acceptably good at whatever it is, but to be world-class you not only have to have talent, you also have to sacrifice almost everything to your goal. You have to care about accomplishing it to the extent that you are willing to give up not only your own other interests, but you may force your closest friend or lover to make the sacrifices too.

When Doug gave me that pedometer in 1979, I was seventy-four, but he gave it to me with a grin, saying, "I'll bet you'll be running marathons when you're eighty!" He may have been thinking of Helen Klein, but I have been a disappointment to Doug. I never cared enough about exercise to work hard at it. I have my own over-riding addiction: writing. Writing this book is a good example of how an irresistible impulse to accomplish something sweeps everything away that obstructs it.

But I must tell you about the pedometer because if you decide walking is for you, you might want to get one. It is a serious decision, for the pedometer will soon influence you more than you expected. When I put it on I began by doing a brisk half mile, but the pedometer led me on to do three-quarters of a mile the next day, and before I knew it I was rounding off a mile! That pedometer has a sneaky way of coaxing us to do a little bit more.

I found another tool to help me. I felt silly at first, but Doug pointed out that everyone was wearing running shoes, even if they are only going to the grocer's, and I soon noticed that this was true. So I gathered up my courage. When I put on a pair of those beautiful stream-lined running shoes, I felt I was presumptuous. I knew I wasn't going to run, not even one step, but when I walked across the floor in the shoe store, I found there was some-thing different in the balance of these shoes. They seemed to tilt forward, to make me move easier, and when I tried them on the Bike Path, it was as if the shoes were walking my feet for me! I thought at the time that I would never wear my running shoes to the grocer's, but now I wear them everywhere. I have a foolish idea they protect me from falling.

I so enjoy my walks! Getting out of the house, walking freely, walking alone, greeting the other regular walkers who ask where I'd been if I skip a day. It is another country, so unlike my quiet home.

I think I'll give you an entry from my journal for November 9, 1982:

The thermometer was 42° and there was a stiff wind from the North; the sky was covered with threatening grey clouds.

I tied a red bandanna over my head and tucked a rain-hat into the pocket of my windbreaker. I wore heavy "loden" cordu-roy work pants, and pulled on, for the first time this year, woolen gloves. (I got them in Estonia almost fifty years ago!) I started off at 7:15.

I decided to measure the distance (with my pedometer) from Second Street East to the cattle guard on Ghericke Road. I thought it would be almost exactly three miles. (It turned out to be 2.8.)

It was a cold walk, but I moved along fast and didn't notice the distance as I sometimes do. The weather provided much to see, not only the clouds moving steadily along the sky and the birds soaring on the currents of the wind, but the change that the cold had brought to the vineyards, which were now the color of tapestries, mostly a burgundy. One vineyard, not yet harvested, had heavy bunches of blue grapes hanging among the dark crimson leaves.

Along Ghericke Road the magnificent, towering eucalyptus were crashing and roaring as the wind ploughed through them, stripping two- and three-foot slabs of bark from their trunks. Many were now smooth, massive warm-honey colored poles supporting the heavy leafy branches. Two were stripped down to pale grey with pinkish tones, so smooth and beautiful I was tempted to stop to stroke them, but I remembered being told that eucalyptus often lost their tops to a high wind, so I hurried past the tossing trees. (Silly goose!)

I came to that slope where rabbits are often playing around their brambly home. The heavy rains of the last two days had covered the slope with fresh grass, a soft sage-green. Even the dry moss on the valley oaks had outlined their branches with the sparkling green of new growth. The rabbits were nowhere to be seen and I thought of them cozily comfortable down below in their burrows.

I met the friendly man who lives near the cattle guard. He was walking his dachshund on a leash and the small dog lunged forward, barking furiously at me. When we stopped to greet each other, he told me his dog, who was wearing a trim red jacket, was named Garibaldi.

Then, having left my friend to return to his house, just as I turned around at the cattle guard, I saw through the woods, on the far side of the stream, a cocoa-brown deer, a mule deer, trotting along the edge of the hillside. It made me remember Vermont deer, whose ears are so much smaller. Vermont rabbits have smaller ears than California rabbits, too. California rabbits look as if their ears were an adornment, not just a useful organ.

As I write this, I feel happy, remembering that good walk.
I hope, when you're old, you'll try walking. It's so easy and does so much for you, both mentally and physically.

In 1990 I read a report from Boston, picked up by the *Los Angeles Times*, that I have kept as a talisman. It was a small group of 90-year-olds described in the article as "frail," living in a nursing home, who were willing to try "weight-lifting" to improve their mobility and strength. Over a period of eight weeks, "two of the patients who had walked with a cane, could manage without; one could rise from a chair without using his arms for the first time in years; and five of them walked fifty per cent faster than before. All were more mobile, had better balance and had suffered fewer falls since the training began."

The news report goes on to say that Evan Hadley, chief of the geriatric branch at the National Institute on Aging, said, "This could greatly reduce the need for nursing home admissions by maintaining the mobility of older people and thus their ability to live independently."

There were only ten people in this experiment, but I find it extremely encouraging. The headline was "SENIORS PUMP IRON, DON'T SWALLOW IT!" I'd like to try it myself; I know I could benefit from it. It's painfully apparent to me these days that I exercise my brain a good deal more than my body. It's this book I blame it on! I don't seem to have time for both.

SUMMING UP: It's clear, isn't it? Keep your muscles moving, and please, all of you, balance your activities. Don't go overboard in one area and neglect another. And don't be so serious that you forget to do things for fun. (That's one precept I follow myself; I am about to cut off this chapter because we have been asked out to lunch.)

⌀

CHAPTER SIXTEEN

Eating—and
Three Helpful Cookbooks

OLLOWING ALONG WITH THOUGHTS about our bodies, the
next thing we should consider is how we nourish
them. I'll begin by telling you about my sinful past.
I'm afraid you will be horrified.

Early on I acquired a taste for deep-fried doughnuts,
roast beef swimming in fatty gravy, and the lovely crackly
skin of the Thanksgiving turkey. I just didn't know any
better because my family never talked about cholesterol or
carcinogens. My family never spoke aloud the word cancer, even when a family member was dying of it. Naturally, I never wondered if the food I was eating contributed to my health; I thought only of how it tasted.

I can remember coming home from school "the long
way" so I could stop by the bakery to get lovely flaky rolls
of puff pastry stuffed with real whipped cream. I can still
feel it melting on my tongue

When I was older, working in John Wanamaker's
book department in New York, I would dart across the

street at lunch time to Child's Restaurant where I would get two large, doughy "butter cakes" that would make me feel full until I got home for a late dinner that night. (John Wanamaker's has long since vanished from Manhattan and perhaps Child's has too, though that white-tiled restaurant survived long enough for me to read later that Gurdjieff, when he was in New York, habitually met his followers there!)

You can see I wasn't giving any thought to nourishing my body, though I was living a hectic life, walking a mile to the railroad station early in the morning, jumping off the train in Jersey City, running to catch the ferry, and then trotting up the steps of the elevated railroad in New York to get to Wanamaker's by 8:30, with the reverse procedure at night, trudging wearily that last mile for a dinner kept warm (and dried out) in the oven of our coal stove.

I didn't pay any attention to the twinges of my teeth when they finally began to protest against the meager nourishment they were being given. It took nearly five years for the neglect of my teeth to catch up with me and by then I was married. We were living in El Salvador where the dentists were not exactly reliable, so today I am very lucky that I haven't one artificial tooth among the ones I was born with.

And I smoked.

While I was in high school I began filching my father's heavy, oval Egyptian cigarettes, smoking away from home, of course. When I graduated from high school, I was so disappointed when my father told me I couldn't go on to college, I exploded, "Well, Dad, then I'm going to get a job and I'm going to smoke in front of you!" I was sixteen.

Cigarettes were cheap then and everyone smoked. I soon worked my way up to a pack a day, but somehow I never, or rarely, exceeded that amount. I didn't like the taste my mouth developed after I had chain-smoked all evening.

It took me a long time to stop smoking. It is, as you know, an addiction like any other, working on its victims both psychologically and physically. I can still remember that lovely deep pull on a cigarette and the feeling as the nicotine went down into my lungs. I used to think I couldn't write if I wasn't smoking. I smoked for forty-five years. I tried stopping once or twice, but it never held. In the end I tried to protect my lungs by using a long Dunhill cigarette holder with a filter inside. This showed me, when I changed the filter, just exactly how much nicotine could have gone into my lungs. I knew, too, that the filter wasn't 100% efficient.

I have two sons. When I came home after two years in Turkey I found one of them, John, was smoking even more than I. When I protested about his smoking, John said gently, "I don't mind people who don't smoke suggesting I stop, but people who smoke. . . ." He let his sentence trail off.

I found then, to my surprise, that I cared more for my son's well-being than my own. I stopped smoking at that moment.

Well, I just about stopped. I thought at first I could have one cigarette after dinner, but I found this made me want to keep on. I remember once at a New Year's Eve party I thought I could celebrate with one cigarette, but I was a true addict; I had to quit cold turkey and I finally did. (John didn't follow my example right away, but he stopped in his own good time.)

If you are serious about enjoying your old age, throw away that cigarette, stamp it out, burn up the pack, and begin a new life.

If you are not a smoker, you can congratulate yourself that you are spared the cruelest obstacle in the path toward a pleasant, comfortable old age.

You may be expecting me to tell you what you should eat and what you shouldn't, but there is no need for me to do this. We are constantly bombarded with advice about our diets. Even the manufacturers are stressing "low fat" and "no additives." It will be quite easy for you to move from a dangerous diet to a safe one, to protect yourself from cholesterol build-up and other harmful substances. You will find it no hardship, not at all like giving up smoking.

You may be interested in how I am handling this problem. I began thinking about it way back in 1972 when I picked up a cookbook, *Diet for a Small Planet* by Frances Lappé. After I read that, in the United States, it takes sixteen pounds of grain and soy beans to produce one pound of beef, I couldn't comfortably go on eating so much more than my share of the world's food, so I stopped eating beef.

Then I read about the way ham and bacon are processed. I felt it would be better not to eat these foods. When the doctors began talking about cholesterol, I came gradually to my present regime which is limited to chicken and fish and relies heavily on vegetables and fruit.

You, naturally, have to make your own choice as to how far you will go in nourishing your body rather than asking it to handle substances that may be inherently unhealthy or dangerous.

I know that the way I have chosen is the best for me. Frankly, I don't want to get cancer! I don't know how to avoid it completely—my genes may even hide a weakness acquired from my forebears—but I want to cut down on anything that may intensify that danger for me. My old age, so far, has been great and I want to keep it so. I can honestly tell you that I feel better physically and emotionally on my "restricted" diet.

Cutting back on sugar and "empty" calories at the same time has let me maintain the same weight I've had for years. Want statistics? I am about 5'5" (when I stand up straight which, nowadays, is only when I remember to do it) and I weigh 130 pounds. (I weighed myself this morning so I could tell you exactly.) That's okay, isn't it?

I'm not a fanatic. I have a glass of sherry before dinner, I eat an oatmeal cookie when I feel like it, but I must admit that I have moved from ice cream to frozen yogurt, and found this no sacrifice.

At any age, being healthy makes all the difference, but as we get older, it's a prize worth working for. And there is a corollary to the advice that you must be responsible for taking care of yourself; taking care of yourself goes beyond giving your body the nutriments it needs.

Do you remember the Peanuts cartoon I spoke about earlier? It has Snoopy waiting for his dinner and remarking "I keep in close touch with my stomach!" My advice to you is to keep in close touch with your whole body. You should learn to listen to it, hear its signals of discomfort. By doing this, I have developed an unexpected self-confidence; I have begun to feel that I understand my body, or at least know more about it than someone who doesn't live in it. This has progressed to where, if I don't trust the advice a doctor gives me, I change doctors.

Let me tell you a story. When I was living in that little house in the woods with the birds and the chipmunks, I had begun to think seriously, as you know, about my future, and I began to notice my body. My left shoulder suddenly became very painful. It turned out to be bursitis and a doctor cured it with a single shot of cortisone. Later, when we had moved to Bennington, the same shoulder began to complain bitterly again. I knew what to do. I went to an orthopedist who gave the expected cortisone shot, but this time it didn't work. The surgeon then told me that my shoulder joint was worn out. I was in my sixties at the time and I didn't feel that old. I refused the new shoulder he offered me.

My friends were surprised when I went to an acupuncturist in Massachusetts, but he cured the bursitis in two treatments. (I'll admit I too was rather surprised, as well as pleased.) That was more than twenty years ago. My shoulder has never troubled me again.

It was about then I started taking calcium to strengthen my bones. I understand that now there is a difference of opinion about the usefulness of calcium in preventing osteoporosis and such tragedies, but I can't help thinking that perhaps it's because of my daily intake of calcium that I haven't broken any bones in my occasional falls in the last decade.

When we first arrived in California, we became aware of Dr. Linus Pauling and his work with Vitamin C. You have probably learned by now that Dr. Pauling was just the type of man to appeal to me and I began taking C and followed his advice on other vitamin supplements. Our bathroom closet door still has a yellowed clipping, "Pauling's 12 steps to health."

Since I am riding all my hobby horses one after another, I am going to include one more. This is my personal objection to women feeling that they must be thin in order to feel "fashionable" or to be admired. I feel that being heavy is a nuisance; your body is a bit awkward and you don't get around easily, and if you are very heavy, you may get comments from almost anyone. But still I think you should consider your wishes, not what others think about you. If you want to, go ahead: be fat!

I recorded in my journal a conversation along this line while we were still in Vermont in the '70s:

My friend: " I am a compulsive eater. It comes from feeling insecure, I think. I have a constant craving for food."

I: "But you should feel secure now. Relationships give security as nothing else can, except, of course, you yourself. And you have a good relationship, don't you?"

M.F.: "I'm afraid I have established the habit of eating more than I need."

I: "It's possible to re-educate your eating habits. It's uncomfortable but it's possible."

M.F.: "Well, I'd better! Women always get fatter as they get older and I'm fat enough right now!"

I: "Oh, don't think of it in that way—being fat or not being fat! What you really have to do is to and get a clear perspective on food."

I added at the bottom of the page: *I should listen to what I'm saying!*

That was in 1973, and I was trying to adapt my own food habits to what I had learned from Frances Lappé, but I wasn't being wholly successful.

Of course, that is just going back to my earlier advice, be inner-directed, not outer-directed!

Just one more thing about your eating habits.

Everyone agrees, I imagine, that the first thing in achieving a happy old age is to be healthy, and this begins with a serious concern with nutrition.

However, I know some people who are no longer young—I should remind you I consider we're no longer young when we reach eighty—and these friends of mine do not forego their pork chops and lemon chiffon pie just to cut down on their cholesterol intake, but when I notice this I make no comment.

I make no comment for several reasons: it's their own decision, not mine; they are good friends and I admire them. But above all, I don't comment because I think our attitude toward life is more important than our diet.

These friends, who are in their eighties, eat food every day that is not contributing to their health, but on the other hand, though they have to get up slowly, and go down steps carefully, they walk two miles every morning. The rest of the day they go to choir rehearsal, delivering meals on wheels, and volunteering at the Senior Center. If they have infirmities, they don't give them first priorities in planning their days.

I have heard people say, "We are what we eat," and I suppose in a way that is literally true, but I am afraid no diet is going to make me public-spirited, altruistic or unselfish.

So when my friends order another cup of coffee (while I sip "Decaf") I don't silently criticize them. The truth is that if I thought adopting their eating habits would turn me into a person who thinks of other people first, rather than "When can I get back to my typewriter?" I'd happily start eating pork chops and french fries.

SUMMING UP: The way to know what to eat is to let your body tell you. The more aware you are of how your body is reacting, to food, exercise or any other activity, the more likely you are to be healthy.

✑

It Pays to Take
the Long View

L ATELY I HAVE BEEN ABSORBED in thinking about the
importance of how we feel about the world (I've
gone far beyond whether we should choose pork
chops or tofu) and how we feel about our own personal
roles in it. Are you concerned only about yourself and
your future, or are you interested in what happens to your
country or, going further, what happens to the world?
You might find it interesting to explore your own attitude
toward life; too often we are unaware of what our actual
objectives are.

But now I must force myself to drop this fascinating
subject, and focus on a smaller segment of it: the attitude
an older person should consciously adopt if his/her later
years are to be rewarding, which is our goal, isn't it?

As long ago as when I was living in those New Hampshire woods, I wrote in my journal:

October 19, 1967. Mine is not a popular view among my contemporaries. I feel, however, that it is positively dangerous to hold to the opinions we acquired forty years ago.

With life being prolonged every year, we in our sixties may easily live to our nineties. (My mother right at this moment is ninety-two.) If we are preparing to be out of step with the world for thirty years, we are preparing for thirty years of isolation and bitterness. I myself do not want to be stuck away in some old-fashioned home here on earth, when all the young people go up to settle on the moon or Venus.

I'm no brain. Walter Cronkite on his 20th Century program can lose me in five minutes. A doctor-friend has explained over and over about the alphabet chain of whatever they are, and, while he is talking, I think I understand, but I never can explain it to anyone else the next day. But I keep trying to understand. At least I'll recognize the new language when I hear it. Well, I hope I will!

The thing is that if you are to be fully alive and active, to be a part of the world you will be living in, you will have to forget what you were taught as a child: "Write Grandma a thank-you letter; don't keep people waiting; be on time! Keep in touch with home by writing regularly." Of course people don't do these things any more.

The way I see it, the first rule is to be open to new ideas, to be non-judgmental. Don't ask the younger generation to follow the rules you learned so many years ago. Any change is hard to accept as you grow older. One of the hardest for me to accept was that perfectly nice young people were living together without plans to get married. But of course I accepted it because I had to; otherwise I'd have lost their friendship.

It is much easier to cling to your past values, to judge everybody and everything by the standards you have always trusted, but if you do, you will be left on the side lines. The future will pass you by, and you will be sitting in your rocking chair, grumbling and complaining with all the other old codgers.

I feel I can't say this too often; an open mind will take you further than you think. It will let you enter the next age of ideas that are continually developing. If you are willing to give them a hearing, you will be able to talk to your grandchildren about things you don't understand at all, and your horizons will be noticeably broadened.

Now I want to ask you to think about the emotional compass you will need for this journey. You may find your compass is already fixed on "true north" because the very fact you are considering how to make your seventies, eighties or nineties pleasant and cheerful is more than half the equipment you'll need. Being aware of your goal is an enormous help, but you need also to be aware of both your handicaps and your assets.

For instance, are you still weighed down with the superfluous baggage laid on your shoulders in your childhood? You may have noticed that a good many people cling to early disappointments, remembering their mother didn't seem to love them, or, later, their young lover betrayed them. Have you recognized that you have been free for some time to make your own judgments, to acknowledge your mistakes were not made by someone else, but by yourself? There are even people who enjoy their grievances, wallowing in self-pity. God forbid that you are in this group. (I once heard someone say that self-pity is the most destructive element loose in the world!)

It is difficult when one is young to accept the long view, but if you can adopt it, you will be spared many minor bruises.

I remember how, when I was young, I wanted everything and wanted it right away. I can't tell you what has changed me, perhaps the simple aging process, but now I can see from a wider perspective. Of course I am aware my days are numbered and my time is short, and it's true I feel a sense of hurry. I don't like to waste time on "entertainment" or boring people. There's so much I want to do in the time I have left. Thus it seems strange that I don't want to cram my remaining days with pleasure and fun, but I have gone the other way. I think it's due to that word I just used, *perspective*. What is important and what is not important has changed for me.

I find this in my journal of 1988:

I have discovered that when my indulgent husband wants to do something, or go somewhere, though I had hoped to get at my typewriter, unexpectedly, without willing it, the whole universe flashes into my mind. I see outer space and all those stars and planets and feel the endless time that surrounds it—and us—so I go with my husband to do what he wants, without feeling disappointment. If I suggest a cheese soufflé, which he makes superbly, but he wants to work on his Turkish translation, then I make macaroni and cheese. It seems to take no energy to ˆagree wholeheartedly. Food can be a pleasure, but it's not one I dream about! I think what I'm saying is that if things don't work out as I would like, it's rarely important and if they do go my way, it's pure serendipity!

I don't always hold up the universe as a backdrop for my recurrent problems or frustrations, but I do try to avoid taking them too seriously. I was brought up to be on time for an appointment. This was drilled into me so indelibly that to this day I am usually early for an appointment and, as I wait for my friend or my dentist or a late guest for tea, I have learned to tell myself I would have wasted that five or ten minutes anyway.

I try not to fuss over trivial nuisances. Have you ever timed a traffic light? Once, when I was in a hurry, the green light abruptly turned to red. Furious, I timed it. Two minutes! I calmed down; why get hot and bothered over two minutes?

You may think these are petty problems, but the way you handle them is a critical part of your attitude toward life. Small problems confront you much more often than large ones.

I suggest you try to be aware of how you've been expending your energy lately. A positive attitude works every time over the negative. It not only puts you in a good frame of mind but it's habit-forming. (You might remember that negative thinking is also habit-forming.)

From time to time I get bogged down in trying to foresee the future. I can imagine all sorts of difficult problems may be waiting for me. I start trying to figure out how I'll manage if I become so ill I have to enter a nursing home. If I'm lucky, I will remember at that point that my worst predictions of disaster have never materialized, that, in the long run, I have been exceptionally lucky, so I tell my overactive mind, "Let's go to sleep. It's not going to get that bad, at least not right now!"

And then, quite often, I get an encouraging dream that calms my forebodings. I had one of those dreams, a rather practical one, just before we left Vermont for California, while I was working on that Foreign Service book. Only now, however, has it become relevant.

My younger friends have been telling me that writing this book would go faster, even easier, if I got myself a computer or a word processor.

I used to think I couldn't write if I didn't have a cigarette in my mouth. Now I am convinced that I can't write if I don't use my pad and pen and then try out the result on the typewriter.

However, my younger son, John, presented me with a computer the other day. *Fait accompli!* I wouldn't let him install it in my workroom. It sits uncomfortably in the guest room, quite out of place. I will bring it out to my workroom when I can type on it as fast as I type on my IBM Selectric. So far, I am nowhere near that speed.

But this morning I came across this 1977 dream, so I have hope that things may change.

March 2, 1977: I had a very encouraging dream night before last. I dreamed I was using a typewriter in front of a large board set with light bulbs, sockets, switches and complicated mechanisms. I was typing away when I made a mistake and then panicked. Lights had come on across the board and there was a loud buzzing.

Then a voice said, from inside the board itself, or behind it, "Don't worry! I can tell you how to fix it; just move that switch, touch this button, press that key, and look, it's all put in order!"

I was amazed to hear a voice from the switchboard but greatly relieved, and when I made a second mistake, the kind voice again told me how to repair it.

Doesn't this sound just like a computer? Well, so far I haven't heard "a kind voice" but I hope that nevertheless the computer and I will soon be talking to one another. As I write, I am only playing with it, arguing with it and laughing at it, though I can't wait until I can really make use of it.

However, to be serious, there is one more aspect to "taking the long view," and that is looking ahead realistically.

Anyone who is reading this book is already thinking about the future, but I must confess that, when we were entering our fifties, neither my husband nor myself had the faintest idea that we didn't have all the time in the world ahead of us. We didn't even consider that many people were forced to retire at sixty-five, which was only fifteen years off for us. We never guessed that once you're past fifty, time accelerates; it simply flies by at an unbelievable rate. Probably you can't believe this, but I'm sorry to say, you will find that it is true.

Let me tell you how foolish we were.

When Fred retired at fifty, having served in the Foreign Service twenty-five years, he didn't want his special training to be wasted, especially as he thought Turkey was not generally known to be the modern, friendly, admirable country it was.

Fred applied to the Graduate School at Princeton, planning to have a second career teaching Turkish Studies. Princeton required him to obtain an M.A. before he went for the Ph.D. he needed to teach in a college or university. He began studying at Princeton in the fall of 1954 and he received his Ph.D. in the spring of 1960. Five and a half years had gone by! This meant, really, that he had only ten years to teach before he would be expected to retire for the second time.

He squeezed into those short ten years four years at the University of Utah, two years in Turkey on a Fulbright grant interviewing Atatürk's former colleagues, and a year in Memphis teaching at Southwestern-at-Memphis. As you know, he ended up in New Hampshire where we lived in the woods with the chipmunks and squirrels. He was teaching at Nathaniel Hawthorne College but too soon his professional life was over. It had flashed by like a comet. His ride on that comet was over before he felt it had really begun. Fred was made Professor Emeritus and he was out.

I'm sure you know that I am not saying you are *old* at sixty-five, but it still seems not to be totally accepted that a sixty-five-year-old has a lot of mileage left in her/him. The trick really is not to let yourself believe you're on the shelf, past your prime, even incompetent; that is: old! You yourself haven't changed at all and the only thing you have to do is to prove, at least to yourself, that you are still capable of doing a worthwhile job. It's your task to find that job, whether it's a paying job or whether it is fulfilling some long-held dream. Just, please, when you reach sixty-five, don't sit down to rest. Keep moving! Take the long view and realize you have a good many years left and you can put them to use.

SUMMING UP: It would even be a good idea to look ahead in earnest right now. You could make some plans. You could even make a serious examination of where you are right now and where you hope you will be, say, five years from now, thinking not only geographically, but also how, for instance, you will be doing with meditation.

CHAPTER EIGHTEEN

⁊

What's Good About Being Old?

I'VE JUST MADE MYSELF A PARALLEL LIST of the advantages and disadvantages of being no longer really young. Believe it or not, the list of advantages is longer than the opposite number. You're surprised? That's because the advantages aren't readily recognized. Let me tell you some of them.

I think I'll begin with a quote from Norman Cousins. I found it in his preface to a book edited by Pat York that she calls *Going Strong*.

Norman Cousins wrote, "A full and rewarding life after sixty-five is commonplace." That's in the "plus" column, isn't it? But he added something for the other side: "The worst thing about being seventy-five is being treated as a seventy-five-year-old. People as a whole have yet to catch up with the fact that the increase in longevity—from forty-four to seventy-four since the turn of the century—has been marked by a corresponding prolongation of good health and intellectual acuity."

Apparently this attitude is worldwide. I have just had a letter from a Turkish friend who lives in Ankara. (Luckily for me, she taught English all her adult life, so our frequent letters go back and forth in English.) Düriye echoed Norman Cousins when she commented that what bothered her was the way people reacted to the normal activities of older people as something remarkable.

I had written Düriye that apparently people were surprised when I had no trouble having my driver's license renewed just before my eighty-eighth birthday. Düriye commented that people mean well but she found it irritating to be told "I am wonderful because I have cooked dinner for a couple of friends."

She had just had a letter from a Swedish friend who, in her eighties, had bought herself a new car, for which she was being criticized. She wrote that, nevertheless, she was going ahead with plans to buy all new living room furniture for her own pleasure because she felt older people should enjoy life. She was expecting more criticism. Düriye added, "I had thought this was an Oriental custom, but I see they have it not only in Sweden but in America, too!"

She ended her letter, "Anyway, dear Rebecca, let's hope we both go on the same way to the end!"

And you, who are reading this, please join Düriye and me in ignoring the "at your age" remarks and the suggestions that we should change our behavior.

There are so many reasons to enjoy our lives as we get older. I suppose it is different with everyone, but I find I put first the independence I have gained. It is a wonderful feeling to know that an ambassadress isn't going to look coldly at me because I have come to tea without a hat. But of course it is more than that. It's being able to refuse to go to cocktail parties, for at cocktail parties I can never have a real conversation with someone because he/she is watching the door to see who else is coming. Diplomatic cocktail parties are boring!

Since Sonoma offers us a good many nice restaurants, I don't have to cook dinner for friends any more; we take them out instead, though I admit I enjoy having people to tea. (I offer them cookies.) I have found tea parties encourage conversation. We often find ourselves exploring subjects no one would ever dream of bringing up at a noisy cocktail party.

There are other advantages to being old. If you have a cold in your head you can lie in bed, comfortably snuffling and coughing, reading a detective story. You don't have to pull yourself together, gathering a supply of Kleenex and aspirin before you leave home to spend a miserable day at your office.

I have another freedom. All those long years in the Foreign Service, I had to wear "suitable" clothes. Now, as I happen to enjoy wearing slacks, I wear them. I feel more comfortable if my legs are covered—they are no longer attractive—and I don't like to wear a short dress, continually pulling at it, trying to cover my bony knees. As for a long dress, it gets in my way when I dart across the garage to my workroom or to the back yard to hang up the clothes. So I wear slacks, even jeans. I don't trip along on high heels, either. I wear flats or brogues, but mostly I wear running shoes. No one seems to mind.

But if you *like* dresses and high heels, be independent, wear them! Whatever you do, dance to your own tune. Here is your chance to do what you want, regardless of what people may think.

One of my good friends, Bari, was a ballet dancer and literally danced her way around the world. Bari retired from the ballet and is now settled here in Sonoma.

When she was seventy-nine, she was taking part in a toe-dancing class. An unfortunate slip brought her to the hospital with a broken pelvis. She told me with a grin that the nurses and doctors always entered her room laughing because her chart had told them her age as well as the toe-dancing accident that had hospitalized her. Bari is indomitable; she is now well into her eighties but keeps limber with Tai Chi. The career she chose may have been glamorous but it was not easy and I imagine it toughened Bari in a way that has helped her through her later years.

Of course we have been talking mostly as if your own old age was a long way off. I think I've told you that it will arrive faster than you think. Anyway, let's face it, one of these days you will yourself suddenly find people think of you as a "Senior Citizen." Whether you are alone or have a companion, you will find that your situation has changed.

I am surprised to find that I realized this in 1967 when Fred was teaching a year in Memphis. This was my first contact with southern viewpoints and way of life; my Memphis journal is a fat one. On October 30, 1967—soon after we had arrived, I wrote in it:

Our contacts with the "outside world" here are so superficial! It's as if we were living on an island. This wouldn't have happened if we still had our children with us. They would have been a liaison, swimming across the water to the mainland to school, bringing friends home with them. They would have carried the cables that fastened this island to the mainland. Now we must consciously construct them by reaching out to those we meet.

And when I'm really old, will it be like this? Will I be on an island, isolated and lonely? Or will I do as I plan now? Will I reach out to people—strangers? Reach out to everyone I meet?

And at the same time will I use my solitude to look deeper into myself, to understand myself, to learn what I believe, for instance?

Perhaps the physical aspects of old age, the sudden fatigue, the poor eyesight, the unreliability of my muscles will decide my attitude.

That was 1967. Thirty years ago! And I was right and I was wrong. It's possible to build bridges from an island, though it is not as easy as when we were young. And it is possible to refuse to focus on those old age infirmities, of which I have all three.

It was from Memphis that we moved north to New Hampshire, to that little house in the woods where I began to try to ready myself for being old. You know by now what books I read, what exercises I did, what adventures I had. Will it encourage you to know, if you haven't realized it already, that in only a few years I discovered life was opening up for me, rather than closing down? I rejoiced and sang in my Bennington journal:

December 3, 1974: What is this? What's happening? Am I coming alive at sixty-nine? How can it be? What has changed? Why do I feel everyone is my friend? However it has come about, I have harvested a bouquet of compliments. It reminds me of the undeserved praise an embassy wife gave me in Turkey: "I'm very glad we're going to a Turkish village with you because I understand your technique with the women is very successful!"

Technique! It was love. It was seeing them as human beings. Maybe that's where this change began, because now I don't see people as foreigners, not as competitors, not as antagonists, that is, not in terms of myself but in terms of them. I even try to see what has made them antagonistic to me, trying to see why they are shy (like the Turkish villagers).

It was soon after I made that entry that I decided that it was partly the color of my hair that made the difference. My hair was newly grey. (Of course white hair is better.) The thing is that old women are not threatening to anyone. Once I realized that, I took advantage of it, I began talking to everyone. I remember a summer day in Bennington when I was standing on the curb in the hot sun, waiting for the traffic light to change. A young boy in jeans, hair tousled, joined me just as the light turned, and I said, as we crossed together, not expecting a reply, "Another hot day!" The boy answered easily as if I were his grand-mother, "I'm going fishing, up on the Battenkill!" and I instantly imagined him on the shady bank, the dappled brown water sliding by below. "You'll get a big one, I'll bet" I said. "No stream's better than the Battenkill!" He grinned.

Then "Bye!" he said as he got into a car parked at the curb, waiting for him.

"Good luck!" I called and started up the shady street toward our house, then stepped aside to let a 15-year-old spin past me on his shiny bike. He said, "Hi!" He said it first!

I remember how I felt that day, as if the world had suddenly become a friendly place and that I was accepted in it. I have never quite lost that feeling. It sounds foolish but it has turned out that by now I feel warm, even tender toward almost everyone. I've already told you that I love almost everyone, corny as that sounds. I feel a real concern for their well-being. I remember how Emily Rockwood wrote once, "I feel as if I were grandmother to the whole world!" I can echo that, in my own way.

Loving anyone, or everyone for that matter, has its dangers; you mustn't let it mean feeling their pain if they are suffering. Internalizing the troubles of your lover or your friend, let alone the whole world, will overwhelm you. You should try to be detached. Yes, feel sympathy, feel compassion, do whatever you can to improve the situation, but don't feel the pain in your own body. Keep inviolate a space between you and the sufferer.

You can also remember this when you yourself are in physical or emotional pain. You can learn, if you try, to remove yourself from the scene, putting the pain at a distance. Perhaps it will work only for a minute; but you will get relief for that minute. If your sorrow is keeping you awake, and you can't seem to put it away, somewhere out of sight, try doing a relaxation exercise. Turning on the TV or radio, if you can't keep your mind on relaxing often helps, as it brings the world right into your room and it may put a different perspective on your problem. If all else fails, making yourself do some heavy physical exercise, even in the middle of the night, somehow changes your mood. Whatever you do, I wish you good luck!

On another, but similar subject, you probably already know that it is harder to see someone close to you suffering than to suffer yourself.

Here, too, you should try to detach yourself, detach yourself emotionally, from whatever serious illness or unhappiness is surrounding you. It is perfectly possible to be concerned and loving and yet not let the suffering overwhelm you. This is not being hard-hearted. You will have more strength, you can act more effectively, if you don't draw into yourself those negative feelings that surround you. Think about it; if your roles were reversed, wouldn't you wish the people you care about to be spared the grief of feeling fully your own desperate situation?

You probably have figured out by now, if you haven't realized it earlier, that being able to put any suffering at a distance takes self-discipline. A good deal of what I have recommended to you involves that same quality. I am hoping that you have been as fortunate as I. If you have adopted any of the exercises in *The Well Body Book* or other such suggestions, you may have found, as I did, that suddenly you seem to have acquired patience, and self-control. I think it was Gurdjieff who started me off on self-discipline. One of my earliest practices—I have told you before—was to do a difficult thing every day; I am still trying to do it. And I think more about the universe and our place in it, my place in it, than I think about the worn furniture in our living room. It's surprising how this simplifies my life!

Long ago, I copied out a quote from Thoreau that E. B. White had used in a letter to a friend (*Letters of E. B. White*, edited by Dorothy Lobrano Guth) (What a great team, E. B. White and Thoreau!)

The quote: "I learned this at least by my experiment [Walden] that if one advances confidently in the direction of his dreams, and endeavors to live the life which he has imagined, he will meet with a success unexpected in common hours." This seems to be true, more often that not. I hope it encourages you!

SUMMING UP: I hope I have persuaded you that being old has definite advantages, because I can assure you, you're going to find them when you get there.

CHAPTER NINETEEN

ℒ

For an Old Friend, Reg Robinson

I MET REG IN THE 1950s, when he, like our oldest son, Doug, was in his late teens. The first time I laid eyes on him, he was hastily mowing the long grass around the cottage we were moving into to spend our first summer in northern Vermont.

Reg later introduced Doug to the best swimming hole ("The Sliding Pools"), the most challenging nearby mountain (Mt. Hunger), and the most attractive girls in the neighborhood. He was a good friend. A few years later, he and Doug decided to perform their required duty to their country, and went down to Montpelier from Maple Corner to enlist in the army. They suffered through basic training together before they were assigned in different directions.

Reg, on leaving the army, got a job with the telephone company, built himself a modern log cabin, married and now has seen his three children through college. Perhaps because of his familiarity with the telephone, for the last fifteen years Reg has called from Vermont to Sonoma to get news of our family.

Reg has become impressed by the fact that the years are catching up with him. When he asked what I was doing and I told him I was writing a book about coping with old age, he shouted across the continent, "Mrs. Latimer, I need that book!"

When Reg calls we always talk about our families and the Good-Old-Days-in-Maple-Corner. So I don't know what he is interested in, what books he reads, nor what path he has taken as he has gone through life. It seems likely that he has never been exposed to the idea of visualization and imaginary doctors. Most people haven't. Indeed, there may be many people who, leafing through this book, feel that these things are not for them. I'd hate that, but more especially, I'd hate for Reg to look for help from me and not find it.

So let me tell Reg and anyone else who is interested, there are several fairly simple things that would be helpful as you get older. There's no reason why you can't handle your later years with ease and perhaps even with pleasure, without going into visualization or "traveling through your body."

The first thing to do is to sit down with a pad and pen to write down what you really want to do with the rest of your life. If you've gotten hold of this book in time, make your list before you retire. But in any event, it's never too late to make your list. You must give it very serious thought.

Be practical! Don't write down, "Live in Hawaii the rest of my life," unless you have already saved enough money to do that, or have a sound idea for making your livelihood in some pleasant way after you have gotten to Hawaii. Of course, if you are not yet retired and really want to laze on Hawaii's beautiful beaches the rest of your life, you could begin saving for that right now.

On the other hand, if you've always wanted to be a ham radio operator, helping out in a disaster or having fun talking to yachts sailing across the South Pacific, you should look now into what you would need in the way of equipment and start studying for the examination for your ham radio operator's license.

If you're a woman and you've always wanted to quilt an heirloom bedspread for your daughter, you can begin collecting books on quilting and even try a few experimental stitches right now.

In other words, think, plan and prepare for the coming challenge.

The thing to remember is that when you "retire," you are free! You can do whatever you want. If you've always wanted to paint, here's your chance. A friend of mine, who spent her life in New York City reading manuscripts for publishers, moved out to Bucks County, Pennsylvania, wrote a book and began to paint. She found she enjoyed painting more than writing and, indeed, became very good at it.

Of course if you have always wanted to try your hand at serious photography, make sure you have a good camera when you stop work, and then go to it. You could decide to go into a special branch of photography—portraits, pets, children, or, like my husband, focus on the incredibly beautiful clouds that usually float by unnoticed.

You're lucky if you are a writer. I can testify that writing is exciting, it is rewarding, it is a challenge every time you lay a blank page in front of you, take your typewriter cover off or turn on your word processor. But if you're a writer, you already know all that.

Even if you're not a writer, you might try writing a journal. Begin one right now, before you enter the new world of retirement. A journal is like the finger exercises of a pianist; as a pianist's fingers learn to fly, your words will begin to flow. A journal can be about anything, of course: descriptions of people you've just met, interesting incidents, your plans for the future, your garden, or your life.

The only thing I don't recommend is a journal in which you record your aches and pains. There are people who write journals that are just one long wail! I can't believe this helps anyone and it certainly doesn't lead to creative writing. If you aren't sure how to begin, almost every town has an adult education course offering to show you the nuts and bolts of writing.

One form of writing that is especially appropriate at this time in your life is autobiography. Your children and your grandchildren, and even your friends, will be delighted to hear that you are writing down what you remember of your early life. Times have changed so much in this century that things that seem ordinary to us are astonishing to our grandchildren. They can't believe we grew up without television!

You can tell that I am myself partial to autobiography because this book is basically autobiographical; in addition, one of my earlier books tells about my childhood and my twenty-five years as the wife of a Foreign Service officer.

People often say that Sonoma, California, is a "volunteer town." It actually seems to have more people volunteering to help in some way than in most towns and cities. This is probably because we have a large percentage of retired people here.

I always felt slightly ashamed that I didn't volunteer to do any needed job, but I felt that my job was at my typewriter. Then one day a friend suggested I offer to teach a class in autobiography at the "Senior Center." I couldn't resist and, though that was four years ago, my class is still meeting. Many of them have finished their books but still come to class, because in some amazing way we have become bonded. It's perhaps inevitable that, having laughed and cried over the happy, sad, and exciting events in each other's lives, we are now close friends.

You can see that it was "volunteering" that gave me this unusual experience of making deep friendships with the ten women and men who were in the class. I might add that it has also helped my own writing. I scattered so many red marks across manuscripts that when someone got one back she would wave it in front of the class, "Look what Teacher has done to my chapter!" Checking over the work of the class has made me more careful with my own writing, and going over the basic rules of good writing for them showed me I needed to review them myself. Another thing I learned from my class was that everyone's life is fascinating. Some of our members had more exotic experiences than others, but the ones who had grown up on farms or in small towns also had riveting experiences to write about.

I've come this far and I haven't mentioned money. It's because I don't feel it is the most important of our concerns as we grow older. I speak as someone who hasn't as much money as many of her friends. I feel money is nice but it doesn't answer most problems for me, especially as I grow older. I can't afford to book passage on a cruise ship, but I have a conviction that if I could, I'd come back the same person who had boarded the ship, so I don't mind not going; I find I can learn more by staying right here. (I'm just about to learn to run that computer my son gave me.)

I have long ago lost the urge to "shop." I resist the bombardment of our consumer age, teasing me to buy this or that. I am happy with our little car, though it is not a late model, and I hope it will take care of me till the end of my life. I have grown so fond of my simple clothes that I don't care about being fashionable. My closets seem to be too full and I have begun a system of giving away anything that I haven't worn in a year. I think I told you that I am most comfortable in slacks, so I will confess that in one of my closets there's a dress. I got it for John's wedding some years ago, and I am keeping it in case there is another such emergency. (So many people said to me at that time, "You aren't going to wear slacks to John's wedding!" that I had to give in.)

I have to confess I have one weakness. I buy books, even though our bookcases are filled. I usually buy them from remainder lists. I love remainder lists; I can spend a whole evening poring over one.

Changing the subject, it would be a good idea to get a pet, if you don't have one. A dog is better than a canary, however. A dog will see to it that you get some exercise. In this town, we have pleasant Bike Paths through meadows and along a running creek that is home to egrets and wild ducks. I see many dogs taking their owners out for a brisk walk on the Bike Path.

Of course a cat is a pleasant and undemanding pet, but not as responsive as a dog, not as much company.

I have just written a letter to the President, and sent a copy to the Postmaster General, because they are planning to raise the rate of postage stamps. I gave them what I hope were very good reasons for not doing so. The real reason, however, is that I spend so much money on stamps, I may have to slow down on buying books if they raise the price of stamps.

I write a lot of letters, and I think you should plan to write letters too. I can hear you saying right now, "But I *never* write letters!" and of course, like my good friend Reg telephoning across the continent, the younger generation uses the phone. But when you are older, writing letters is like planting a garden; you are rewarded by getting letters back. I'm sure your mail nowadays is mostly bills, political advertising and junk mail, isn't it? You can't imagine how differently you will feel about the mail if among all that rubbish—for you will continue to get it—you find a letter written to you, with only you in mind, a personal letter!

A few of the people you write may not answer. Only one of my grandsons answers my letters, and a granddaughter does when she's not too busy, but I write all of them anyway. However, I generally write to people like myself, older, who will be glad to know how I am doing and invariably respond with their own news.

An important requirement for writing is to arrange a pleasant place for it. A bay window is nice, especially if African violets grow in it. A small desk in your bedroom would do. You could even use the dining room table. I keep a list of the letters I write because my memory isn't what it used to be and I can't always remember when I last wrote Pam or Christie. Keeping in touch with your old friends is truly essential. You don't want to lose them, for then you will lose a part of your past.

But I do have a warning about one aspect of remembering your past; that is, clinging to it. When we are really old—remember Emily Rockwood said we aren't really old until we are ninety—but when we reach that age there seems to be a tendency to lose ourselves in the past, to dwell in memory on our childhood. You may not be aware that you are glamorizing those early days, but from your distance they will appear idyllic. You may spend a lot of time daydreaming about them.

Resist that impulse! That was then. This is now! Live in the present, look forward to the future. *What future?* you may ask. Well, it doesn't have to be a distant event, but probably most of us need an attractive carrot to encourage us. So, instead of losing yourself in your memories as you sit in your comfortable rocking chair, get up, go to the phone, make a date for lunch with a friend for the coming week. Even if it's July, you could begin to make out your

Christmas card list. Do whatever it takes to keep moving forward!

There's no need to tell you everyone is different. If you always have been a joiner, your later years are sure to be active. You might even decide to live in a retirement community where the friendly clubhouse, the amateur plays and the constant entertainment will give you as much to do as you could possibly want.

Some people don't go in for joining clubs and groups. I am one of them, but I am lucky because all I need is a workroom and a few close friends.

Since I believe in planning, I have already thought through how it would be if I were left alone. I know exactly what I would do. I would find a little house with two bedrooms—one for sleeping, one for working—and I would hope it would be just around the corner from a friendly restaurant where I could make an arrangement to eat my dinner every night. If you should walk in, the waiter might notice you are looking over at the old lady who is reading a book as she eats her dinner, and he smiles. "She comes here every night," he says. "I don't know who she is." That would be me.

I think that about wraps it up for you, Reg. I hope you are persuaded that planning is the key and that it will be possible for you to live a long time, as they all tell us we're going to do, and enjoy most of it.

SUMMING UP: If you have skipped Chapter 10 because it looked too fantastic (and I guess it *is* fantastic!), I think you'd be wise to go back to have a second look at it. You needn't try the exercises if they seem too bizarre, but please read enough to be persuaded by Dr. Assagioli that your body is not you. And remember it's your body that's aging, not you!

CHAPTER TWENTY

⌀

Death

I AM ABOUT TO BRING UP A SUBJECT that always provokes a strong reaction, usually negative: death. Cynthia, Christie and Pam, and other young people, probably haven't thought about it. When we are young, we simply don't believe we are ever going to die, and though my friends have begun to think about their old age, they may never have looked further—to the day when they are no longer surrounded by this beautiful world of sunshine, blue sky and flowers. Even when one of us is trapped in an unbearable situation, most of us don't think of dying as a way out; we expect the situation to improve.

What will you say when I tell you that I think it's very probable that our life after we die may be better than on this earth?

I'm not picturing us playing a harp while sitting on a soft cloud, but I think it is very possible that we may find we are among congenial companions who will draw us into interesting and useful activities. (I remember Emily Rockwood speaking of the "great adventure," and how she hoped she would be kept busy in the next world; she was tired of the idle life her old age imposed upon her.)

Most people seem to think of the "hereafter" as a place for punishments or rewards—heaven or hell. In my view this is a simplistic, even naïve, concept. I will now make my own simplistic statement. I think it possible that the way we see our present surroundings is a "construct," which is accepted by a majority of the people around us and passed on to their children, though this idea is probably no more based on fact than the idea of heaven and hell. In defense of my theory, I might add that some of our greatest intellects felt something of the sort, as you will see later in a quote from Einstein.

As for our future, I prefer to have an open mind. One of the reasons I think the "hereafter" will not be simple annihilation is derived from the reports of people who have been brought back to life "from death." I will tell you about some of these reports that have influenced me, but first I should tell you how I came to my personal optimism. I came to it slowly.

I have spoken earlier of having heard Alan Watts speak while we were living in Salt Lake City in 1963. At that time I made a "seminal" note in my journal:

Salt Lake. March 5, 1963: Alan Watts spoke. He said, in answer to a question, that he thought the ego didn't survive death, but that the unconscious self, the real self, is part of the cosmos, and therefore survives. This is new to me and it seems a good idea.

I never had the good fortune to hear Alan Watts speak again, but I sought out his books.

It was in 1974 that I had an extraordinary dream that at the time I didn't realize was a clear sign that I was not afraid of death any more. At that time I hadn't even begun to think about leaving this world. I was too busy.

In the dream I was living alone in some vague place. I wandered through the village every day, talking to people, and I often saw old women and always talked to them. One day I came upon an old woman who was very unhappy; she felt she had only a bleak future before her, perhaps a nursing home would be her next move. She told me she thought she might kill herself. I wasn't at all shocked at her suggestion. I thought it sensible.

I had talked earlier to another old woman who had come to the same decision. I told my new friend about her. I had been with Beth when she went out to the edge of the water to drown herself. Thin, pale, frail, she first drew back from the physical act, although emotionally she was quite ready for it. Then she jumped in.

This second old lady said, "I'll do it if you'll come with me."

I knew I had been ready to die for some time, so I said, "All right, I will."

We walked to the edge of the water and jumped in.

The water was horrible, thick, brown, dirty, disgusting. I hated to think of it in my lungs and mouth, but I held my breath and went down, hoping I wouldn't know when the nasty water actually entered my body.

The next thing I knew, the old woman and I were above the water, in the air.

I remembered how I had heard that spirits often clung for a short time to their former life and I thought I'd like to float around a little before I went on.

"Let's see if we can soar," I said, and I moved smoothly up through the air. My friend followed me. Then I saw another woman; it was the one who had drowned herself earlier. She looked not exactly young, but different, eager, though shy. "She looks like herself," I thought. "Come on and try it, Beth," I called, and she rose on her toes, timidly putting herself into the air, and came after us.

When I woke from that dream, I simply recorded it; I didn't try to interpret it, though now it seems very clear to me.

A year later, a relative and friend, who was dying of lung cancer, asked my husband and me to come see him. That was probably the first time I had tried to put into words my idea of life after death.

I wrote in my journal:

I think not everyone clings to the concept of the next world being not unlike our present world, to the concept that we keep our personalities and our bodies. Perhaps those who do will find their heaven—or hell! But those more interested in the possibilities of growth, of change, probably succeed in shaking off the clinging, earthy atmosphere and they proceed on into a different sphere. I can't imagine what this sphere could be but I believe in its existence because I believe that the principle that governs creation is growth and change.

What is it that the Tibetans say? "Watch out when you die! You have to fight your way past the Things that will hold you to the familiar aspects of life." Well, I'm prepared to fight!

(So I was ready to talk about this great subject, but my dying friend kept carefully to superficial topics.)

By the time we moved out to California I had come to feel confident that dying would be a test and a challenge, but one I welcomed. Just before we left Vermont I wrote out my conclusions; I haven't changed them since:

Thanks to William James, Mary Austin, Aldous Huxley and, of course, Alan Watts, I know that when we die we don't just drop over the edge into a void. We move out into space where we even have a choice of what happens to us. It is a space of which we get glimpses while we are here in our bodies, if we are open. The space is not empty. It is occupied by unimaginable entities, concentrated essences of power and light, as well as by simpler manifestations, who are closer to what we are as we live in our bodies. These are the Kindly Greeters, the ones who remember or are still concerned with their earlier existence on earth. They are the ones who are seen by the dying and help awakened souls (Aldous Huxley, for instance) make their way through this first

*area, where it would be easy and pleasant to remain. Beyond is
a more challenging, mysterious area.*

And what will I do?

*I am not a thinker, a philosopher, a scientific explorer, only
a groper, a simple seeker. I have made only the first steps on this
strange road.*

*What will I do when I die? Will I dare to try to get through
the "anteroom?" I don't know, but I hope I will.*

I was surprised when I came upon this passage as I
was writing this book. I didn't remember that I had
sketched out so clearly what I had come to believe. It
seems as if I had tucked it into some secure corner of my
mind and from then on I didn't bother to think about how
it would be in the future because I "knew" I'd be all right.
I feel I was very fortunate.

Of course, it was also the reports of people who had
survived near-death experiences which encouraged me
and I will now tell you about a few of them.

We were living in Bennington, Vermont, when I first
began to notice that people who survived near-fatal experiences seemed to have had an insight into what it was like
to die.

The first example of this was a surprising one. In June,
1974, NBC had an interview with just such a person, a man
who had been revived after a heart attack. *He was a
pleasant, forty-ish man, sensitive,* I wrote in my journal. *The
interviewer asked him, "Did you know it was coming? Was
there pain? Were you frightened?"*

*"I knew something. I said, 'Oh, Lucy,' to my wife and that's
all I could say. There was no pain. I wasn't frightened."* He
hesitated, though he must have been asked the same questions
many times. *"It was as if I had started on a trip."*

"A trip? What was your destination?"

*"I didn't know. I was simply moving on. I can't really
describe it, but it was as if I'd begun a trip."*

"And you weren't frightened?"
'"No, not frightened in the least."
"Before this experience, did you fear death?"
"Yes. I feared it."
"And now?"
"Now I don't fear it, not any longer."
That was a nice report, wasn't it? Not frightened, no pain!

It wasn't long after that I saw an interview on Vermont Educational Television with the well-known authority on death and dying, Elizabeth Kübler-Ross. She was very interesting, of course, but she made one statement that I found extraordinary. I recorded it in my journal:

She said that, being a physician and psychiatrist, that is, a scientist, she could state that after death a person is met by someone loved and missed, or by Jesus or Mary and that every "returned" individual says dying is a beautiful experience.

These, of course, are the "Kindly Greeters" I had heard of before.

I still wonder at this unequivocal statement, though I am, of course, inclined to believe it.

Later I chanced upon a book by Marya Mannes, *The Last Rights*. She quoted a report issued by the Foundation of Thanatology in which some doctors said they had reason to believe that the dying can experience a sense of surrender that borders on ecstasy.

I remember how astonished I was when I read that. My experience, especially when acupuncture cured my bursitis, had made me believe that no doctor could tolerate any belief that wasn't scientifically proven. I thought of this report as a hopeful sign that doctors might not have as narrow a view as I had believed.

Marya Mannes also quoted Einstein—Einstein whom I remembered walking around the streets in Princeton, N.J. as if he were an ordinary person. When one of

Einstein's friends died about a month before Einstein did, Einstein wrote, "Now he's gone slightly ahead of me again, leaving this strange world. That doesn't mean anything. For us believing physicists this separation between past, present, and future has the value of mere illusion, however tenacious. . . ."

One last quote from *The Last Rights:* It is an apt quotation from Emily Dickinson.

"Eternity will be
Velocity or pause,
Precisely as the candidate
Preliminary was."

In 1976 my friend, Bill Elliott, told me about his grandfather who was in his seventies and lived alone. He had had two "heart arrests," and each time was "brought back from death."

His surgeon wanted to do open heart surgery on him, "to give him another ten years," but he refused. His life was complete, he said. Why should he prolong it?

When Bill went home at Thanksgiving, he went to see him. His grandfather said he wanted to tell Bill something he hadn't told anyone, because they would think he was loony.

He told Bill that when his heart had stopped, he'd found himself in a very pleasant place which had a beautiful light. He didn't want to leave it to return to life. And he had the same experience with the second "heart failure." So he was ready to go now, he said. He had no fear.

Bill's story seemed very heartening to me. A simple man, a simple reaction to an extraordinary experience, it rings of the truth.

I didn't come upon *In My Own Way: An Autobiography* by Alan Watts when it was first published, but I found it at about the same time my friend, Bill, told me about his grandfather.

Watts wrote about his friend, Jean Varda, and told his story so well I am scarcely going to cut it.

Varda was a Greek, born in Smyrna, an artist who worked chiefly in collage. He lived on an old ferry boat moored in Sausalito, California and enjoyed life to the utmost. Watts wrote, "[He] lived close to poverty so that he need keep no records, pay no taxes, nor possess resources for which anyone could sue him.

"A year or so before he died he had a stroke. When I saw him the day after, he said, 'Alan, I am afraid to tell this to most of my friends because they will think I am crazy. But I was quite sure I was going to die, even that I was dead. It was astonishing! It was an apotheosis!

"'I found myself somewhere where I and everything else were transformed into a warm, golden light, where there were formless presences welcoming and reassuring me, like angels. How can I say it? All this was much more real than ordinary life, which now seems like a dream, so that I can't possibly be afraid of death any more. Can you understand this?

"'I knew for sure that this golden light, this divinity which I became, is the real thing. That this world in which you and I are talking is just a shadow. That we haven't anything to worry about at all—ever. And my God, how can this have happened to *me?* Alan, you know I am a scoundrel and a lecherous man. What do you think? Am I nuts? Was I hallucinating? If they wouldn't think I was quite mad, I would recommend *everyone* have a stroke.'"

There's nothing more to say, is there?

To be totally realistic, I should add that there is no use worrying about what happens to you after death, (if you are still worrying,) because that won't change anything except your life up to the point of dying, and whatever does happen afterwards will happen, no matter whether you expected heaven or hell—or neither.

SUMMING UP: Two or three years ago I met a young woman who developed an exaggerated notion of who I was. She told me she often wrote down things I said!

So when I awoke from a dream one morning, I knew I was speaking to her when I heard myself saying, "You may weave me an elaborate shroud if you wish, but left to myself, I would leave quietly."

In fact, I will launch myself into death like a bird taking flight for home.

CHAPTER TWENTY-ONE

⌀

Adding It All Up

E HAVE COME A LONG WAY TOGETHER, haven't we? From New Hampshire to California, by way of Vermont. From 1968 to 1994. And we not only have covered space and time, but we have had some amazing experiences along the way. For me, remembering those years has been both wonderful and painful. For you, I hope it has been helpful.

You already know, but I must say it once again, that I haven't expected any of you to follow in my exact footsteps: meditating on a candle, doing autogenic exercises for twenty years, listening to what your wrist tells you about a dancing partner long forgotten. What worked for me may not work for you, but if you keep at it, you will find your own road.

When we started this exploration, I told you I would hold nothing back, that I would describe exactly what I did and what I learned, and I have kept my word. I have left nothing out. I can't tell you, however, exactly which of those experiences resulted in my old age being the best years of my life.

I am sure of one thing, that meditation is the keystone and, in case I haven't yet convinced you, I will give you one final argument in its favor, that I found in the *Noetic Sciences Review.*

"Meditation may have more to offer than a calm mind and lower blood pressure. Recent research in *The Journal of Behavioral Medicine* shows that a simple meditation practiced twice a day for a 20-minute period leads to marked changes in an age-associated enzyme, DHEA-S. Levels of DHEA-S in experienced meditators correspond to those expected of someone 5-10 years younger who does not meditate.

"The enzyme is produced by the adrenal glands, and its level is closely correlated with age in humans. It has also been associated with lower incidences of heart disease and lower rates of mortality in general for males and with less breast cancer and osteoporosis in women."

This study examined men and women who practiced Transcendental Meditation and had done so for ten or eleven years.

The article ends: "Are these salutary changes directly due to 'sitting in meditation'?" According to Joe Glaser, who headed the study, the effect may be because meditators learn to approach life with less physiological reaction to stress. "Whatever the cause," he added, "spending twenty minutes twice a day for a body that is measurably more youthful seems like a fair exchange." I think we all can say *Amen* to that.

As you know, I myself haven't meditated twice a day for twenty minutes, but even my erratic practice must have had some share in my ending up at ninety in good shape. If you are still resistant to meditation, you may discover, as I have, that your resistance lessens as you continue. I find that these days I never miss my daily session. I think that if I were free to do so, I would make my way up through the fragrant redwoods on Sonoma Mountain to sit *zazen* at the Zen Center on the ridge of the mountain.

Being aware comes next in importance to meditation. (Waking-up or self-observation, as Gurdjieff calls it, and the popular writer Thich Nhat Hanh's mindfulness, are all basically the same.)

I haven't come across any new revelations on the usefulness of "waking-up," but I can say that it is an astonishingly addictive practice. If you can manage it for even a minute or two, you will probably find you want to keep on trying. Seeing everything clearly around you, including yourself, is like being blind and suddenly gaining your sight; the whole world is new, bright, and beautiful.

So if you have tried it and discovered it is not easy, just keep on trying. We can train ourselves to do it—to observe ourselves, to recognize the underlying meaning of a desire or the emptiness of a daily routine. Aldous Huxley, in his novel, *Island*, includes a talking bird, a mynah, trained to repeat all day long, "Attention! Attention!" Huxley had the right idea. We all need to be reminded to pay attention, to notice what is actually happening, to hear what we are actually saying, to recognize how we are feeling.

All of us have met up with nice people who are totally unconscious of where they are letting their lives lead them. They are even unaware of what they are feeling until an unsuspected emotion, a need or a hunger leads to a sudden outburst. Being aware will help you avoid that.

The other skills I have learned seem rather humdrum by comparison, but learning to put pain at a little distance, learning to look after my body, learning to relax, through visualization, is not humdrum: Jaime, my imaginary doctor, is witness to that. He is now an important part of my life.

I suppose you have noticed that self-discipline is an integral part of the whole equation. It seems to me that this develops almost without our noticing it, though some of Dr. Assagioli's exercises are obviously directed toward that goal and Gurdjieff's "Do a difficult thing every day," is totally an exercise in self-discipline. Of course, those of you who have been able to stop smoking have demonstrated that you already have acquired superior self-discipline.

I haven't mentioned a tiny aspect of magic that we can take advantage of, but I must not leave it out. Somewhere along the way I picked up the idea that if I refuse negative thoughts and emotions, if I smile rather than frown, laugh rather than cry, my mood changes entirely. The smile and the laugh become genuine. Try it!

If you've stopped to think about it, you will have realized that these wise people you've been hearing about are actually saying the same thing. Details may vary, the exercises they recommend may be different, but essentially they all have been telling us that each one of us has powers that most of us haven't been using, that these powers are available to us if we are willing to give a little time, exert some self-discipline—and temporarily suspend disbelief.

Not one of these extraordinary teachers asks us to take an exercise on faith. We are told to prove for ourselves the truth of what we have been told. Sometimes it may be impossible for us to see any reason for standing on a chair for ten minutes or to take part in Gurdjieff's difficult STOP exercise, but it has been my experience that if I give such challenging suggestions a fair trial, I learn something.

I have already described to you an experience that proved to me personally that faith wasn't necessary for my body to do what I was asking of it. I had read in several books that such a thing was possible but I didn't know anyone who had attempted such a bizarre experiment.

You probably remember the frightening diagnosis of basal and squamous cells inside my nose. When I summoned that "White Army" to rid myself of the cancerous cells, I wasn't even hopeful that I had devised a suitable way to achieve my purpose. In fact, I hadn't the slightest idea I would succeed. It was only desperation that drove me to that visualization twice a day for six weeks. But it worked. Without faith.

Adding it all up, it results in this work of ours consisting of basically only two goals: strengthening and empowering ourselves as we grow old, and once older, how to get the most out of the years that lie ahead of us.

So now let's move on to the practical side of being older. I think the first rule is that we can't cling to old habits and old rules of behavior. I know I have spoken of this before but it needs to be emphasized. I remember clearly that I never once heard that paragon of an old woman, Emily Rockwood, exclaim, shaking her head, "What on earth is the world coming to?"

So please remember that if you can't go along with the crowd, it is best to keep silent. Accept, or at least try to understand, new trends, new discoveries, new use of language, although some of it may seem foolish or useless or even downright disgusting. Believe me, your life will be richer if you can welcome the future as it approaches.

One of the most rewarding things you can do in your older years is to keep in circulation; meeting people, walking, playing golf or bridge. Volunteer wherever help is needed. Take advantage of those days you feel on top of the world to do something new or to make a new friend. If you are forced to be quiet, reach out by telephone or with letters. You may find that a computer can provide more entertainment than a soap opera. You can meet people through your computer as easily as a ham radio operator does, and you don't have to have a license to do it!

One last, serious, word: nearly all the books I've read emphasize that it is almost impossible to go very far on an esoteric route without a teacher and I believe they are right. If you can find a teacher, latch on to him or her. It is safer and easier, and a living guide will dramatically increase the speed with which you move along the road.

SUMMING UP: And so I end what has turned out to be not only addressed to Christie, Pam, Sue and Cynthia, but an open letter to anyone who is looking down at the slippery slope that leads to old age. To all of you, everyone of you, I wish a heartfelt *Good Luck!*

With love,

Rebecca

Recommended Books

N ote: This list is by no means comprehensive. It is made up from the books I have on my shelves and is meant only as a starting point for your own search for helpful guides. I'm afraid that some of them may even be out of print.

Anderson, Walt. 1979. *Open Secrets: A Western Guide to Tibetan Buddhism.* Viking Press, New York.
  I read everything I come across on Buddhism and find something in every one. I found an acceptable translation of "Om Mani Padme Hum" in Anderson's book.

Assagioli, Roberto. 1976. *Psychosynthesis: A Collection of Basic Writing, A Manual of Principles and Techniques.* Penguin/Esalen, New York.

_____1974. *The Act of Will.* Penguin/Esalen, New York.
  These are the only books by Assagioli that I have on my shelves, but they were sufficient for me. I understand that other people have "explained" Assagioli, but I stick to my principle, "Always go to the source, not to anyone else."

Austin, Mary. 1923. *Everyman's Genius*. Bobbs Merrill, Indianapolis, IN.

_____1932. *Earth Horizon: Autobiography*. Houghton Mifflin, Boston.
Mary Austin's books have long been out of print, but I suggest you test the resources of your library. Austin's autobiography is quite as interesting as the book, *Everyman's Genius*, that fired me up years ago.

Boyd, Doug. 1974. *Rolling Thunder: A Personal Exploration into the Secret Healing Powers of an American Indian Medicine Man*. Dell Publishing Company, New York.
A vivid book with many examples of the incredible powers of a shaman.

Brody, Jane. 1985. *Good Food Book*. W.W. Norton, New York.
It is just what it says. An excellent book.

Castaneda, Carlos. 1969. *The Teachings of Don Juan: A Yaqui Way of Knowledge*. Ballantine Books, New York.

_____1971. *A Separate Reality: Further Conversations with Don Juan*. Simon & Schuster, New York.

_____1972. *Journey to Ixtlan: The Lessons of Don Juan*. Simon & Schuster, New York.

_____1974. *Tales of Power*. Simon & Schuster, New York.

_____1977. *The Second Ring of Power*. Simon & Schuster, New York.

_____1981. *The Eagle's Gift*. Simon & Schuster, New York.

_____1984. *The Fire Within*. Simon & Schuster, New York.

_____1987. *The Power of Silence: Further Lessons of don Juan*. Simon & Schuster, New York.

_____1993. *The Art of Dreaming*. HarperCollins, New York.

I bought all of Castaneda's books as they appeared in paper-back. I still find that Castaneda takes a lot of concentration on my part, but I keep stubbornly plowing on. You might look for Daniel Noel's book on this list if you too find Castaneda hard to digest.

David-Neel, Alexandra. 1927. *My Journey to Lhasa: The Personal Story of the Only White Woman Who Succeeded in Entering the Forbidden City.* Harper & Bros., New York.
     This edition has a beautiful binding. I hope you can find a copy of this book for you feel then the very breath of Tibet before it was invaded by the Chinese.

_____1979. *Buddhism: Its Doctrines and Its Methods.* Discus Books/ Avon Books/ Hearst Corporation.
     This book is a translation from the French and is full of interesting facts and explanations.

Green, Elmer and Alyce. 1977. *Beyond Biofeedback.* Delacorte Press, New York.
     This is a riveting book, for though scientific, it is threaded through with magic.

Gurdjieff, G. 1963. *Meetings with Remarkable Men.* E.P. Dutton, New York.
     Peter Brook based his beautiful film on this book. (Gurd-jieff's own account of his early years and his studies with esoteric sects.)

Hamilton-Merritt, Jane. 1976. *A Meditator's Diary: A Western Woman's Unique Experience in Thailand Temples.* Harper & Row, New York.
     A book that gives you every detail of life in a Buddhist monastery. Admiration of Hamilton-Merritt's strength of char-acter and self-discipline is what you are left with.

(De) Hartmann, Thomas and Olga. 1983. *Our Life with Mr. Gurdjieff.* Harper & Row, New York.
     A disarming book. Both the Hartmanns were artists and their account is touchingly modest and sincere.

Hoffman, Edward. 1988. *The Right to Be Human: A Biography of A.H. Maslow.* Jeremy B. Tarcher, Los Angeles.
If you can't get hold of Maslow's Journals, this is the next best.

Hulme, Kathryn C. 1966. *Undiscovered Country: A Spiritual Adventure.* Atlantic Monthly / Little Brown, Boston.
This reads like a novel, but gives the reader genuine insights into how a sophisticated woman can learn from the Gurdjieff experience.

Humphreys, Christmas. 1971. *A Western Approach to Zen.* A Quest Book, the Theosophical Publishing House, Wheaton, IL.
Christmas Humphreys is a well-known authority on Zen and this book is for the serious student who will learn much from it.

Huxley, Aldous. 1945. *The Perennial Philosophy.* Harper & Brothers, New York.
This is a classic that goes to the roots of what we all believe.

_____1962. *Island.* Harper & Row, New York.
An entertaining novel that leaves the reader feeling thoughtful.

_____1969. *The Letters of Aldous Huxley.* Edited by Grover Smith, Harper and Row, New York.
Huxley's letters give the flavor of the man himself.

Huxley, Laura Archera. 1963. *You Are Not the Target.* Farrar, Strauss & Co., New York.
Entertaining but also has some useful advice.

James, William. 1958. *The Varieties of Religious Experience.* Mentor / New York American Library, New York.
First published in 1912, people are still reading it, but have not acted on it.

Jaffe, Dennis T. 1980. *Healing from Within: How to Gain Greater Control over Your Own Health.* Knopf, New York.
Excellent exercises.

Kapleau, Philip, ed. 1967. *The Three Pillars of Zen: Teaching, Practice and Enlightenment.* Beacon Press, Boston.
This book is very readable and informative at the same time.

Lappé, Frances Moore. 1971. *Diet for a Small Planet.* Ballantine Books, New York.
There is a 1982 edition and probably one even newer, but whatever edition, this is a very useful book, as it gives excellent recipes and backs them up with a discussion of why it is better for us to moderate our consumption of food, especially beef.

Lowry, Richard J., Ed. 1979, 2 v. *The Journals of A.H. Maslow.* Brooks / Cole Publishing Co., Monterey CA.
This is really Maslow talking to himself, very revealing of his true character.

Luce, Gay Gaer. 1979. *Your Second Life: Vitality and Growth in Maturity and Later Years.* Delacorte, New York.
This is an astonishing story of what a group of older people were able to accomplish by working together on control of their minds and bodies.

Mannes, Marya. 1974. *Last Rights.* William Morrow, New York.
Frank and outspoken on the problems of aging.

Maslow, A. H . 1971. *The Farther Reaches of Human Nature.* Viking, New York.
It may open your eyes.

_____1968. *Towards a Psychology of Being.* D. Van Nostrand-Reinhold, New York.
If you read *The Farther Reaches,* you will want to read this.

_____1988. *The Journals of A.H. Maslow,* 2 v. Ed. By Hoffman. Listed under Hoffman, Edward.

Noel, Daniel, C., Ed. 1976. *Seeing Castaneda: Reactions to the "don Juan" Writings of Carlos Castaneda.* Perigee Books / G.P.Putnam's Sons.
If you are interested in Castaneda, puzzled by him or fascinated, try to get hold of this book of comments on Castaneda by a variety of people.

Orage, A.E. 1974. *Psychological Exercises and Essays: Over Two Hundred psychological exercises and fifteen essays designed to increase the flexibility and scope of our minds in the ongoing process of consciousness.* Samuel Weiser, Inc. York Beach, Maine.
Orage, an English writer and editor, was one of the most interesting men who joined Gurdjieff's "school."

Ouspensky, P.D. 1971. *The Fourth Way: A Record of Talks and Answers to Questions based on the teaching of G.I. Gurdjieff.* Vintage/Random House, New York.
It was my chief guide in trying to understand Gurdjieff's teachings.

_____1945. *In Search of the Miraculous: Fragments of an Unknown Teaching.* Harcourt, Brace and World, New York.
I have read this many times, understanding each time a little bit more, and picking up new ways to develop self-discipline.

Pelletier, Kenneth R. 1977. *Mind As Healer, Mind As Slayer: A Holistic Approach to Preventing Stress Disorders.* Delacorte/Lawrence. New York.
The writer gives an excellent overview of the various possibilities for taking better care of ourselves.

Ram Dass. 1978. *Journey of Awakening: A Meditator's Guidebook.* Bantam, New York.
A very practical book, drawing on a variety of sources for inspiration and direction.

Reps, Paul, compiler. n.d. *Zen Flesh, Zen Bones: A Collection of Zen and Pre-Zen Writings.* Anchor/Doubleday & Co., New York.
A delightful book and also very practical for the newcomer to meditation.

Robertson, Laurel, Carol Flinders and Brian Ruppenthal, 1986. *The New Laurel's Kitchen: A Handbook for Vegetarian Cookery and Nutrition.* Ten Speed Press, Berkeley, CA.
This book will give you the answers to your questions about taking care of your body with regard to food. The recipes are interesting and draw on many cultures.

Suzuki, Daisetz T., 1962. *The Essentials of Zen Buddhism: Selected from the Writings of Daisetz T. Suzuki.* E.P. Dutton, New York. Bernard Phillips, Ed.
An excellent book.

Samuels, Mike and Hal Bennet, 1973. *The Well Body Book.* Book Works/Random House.
This book is challenging, stimulating and informative.

_____With Nancy Samuels, 1975. *Seeing With the Mind's Eye: The History, Techniques and Uses of Visualization.* Book Works. Random House. New York.
A fascinating book and worth getting for the illustrations alone.

Simonton, Carl, Stephanie Matthews and James Creighton. 1978. *Getting Well Again.* J.P. Tarcher, Los Angeles.
The well-known method of using a combination of medical treatment with visualization to work on cancer.

Smith, Adam, pseud. 1975. *Powers of the Mind.* Random House. New York.
An informal survey which made me go to some of the subjects described.

Tart, Charles T. 1987. *Waking Up: Overcoming the Obstacles to Human Potential.* Shambala, Boston.
This is Tart's "Gurdjieff" book and it's very readable and enlightening.

_____1989. *Open Mind, Discriminating Mind.* Harper & Row, New York.
This gives excellent information on self-remembering.

Van de Wetering, Janwillem. 1978. *A Glimpse of Nothingness: Experiences in an American Zen Community.* Pocket Books. Washington Square Press. New York.
Entertaining and informative.

_____1975. *The Empty Mirror: Experiences in a Japanese Zen Monastery.* Houghton-Mifflin, Boston.

These two books really go together and are an interesting account of van de Wetering's development.

Watts, Alan. 1972. *In My Own Way.* Pantheon, New York.
The way he saw his life when he looked back at it.

◊

The Thanks Be To
Grandmother Winifred Foundation
P.O. Box 1449. Wainscott, New York, 11975-1449

Index

About the Author

FOR TWENTY-FIVE YEARS, Rebecca Latimer travelled the world as the wife of a career Foreign Service Officer. Because of her objection to the Department of State's policy requiring submission and approval of all published material before it could be made public, essentially censorship, she waited a quarter of a century to publish her work. In the meantime, knowing that some day it would be important to remember everything that happened, she recorded her experiences in the privacy of her daily journals. It was only after her husband's retirement in 1954 that Rebecca was able to reveal her charm, wit and wisdom to the world.

Her work has now been published in *The New Yorker*, *Harper's Magazine, House and Garden*, and *Western Humanities Review*. She has also published a children's book titled *Susie and Leyla: Teenagers in Turkey*. Rebecca's journals, letters, manuscripts and other papers have all been reserved for future housing in the permanent "Rebecca Latimer Special Collection" at Mills College Library in Oakland, California.

Born in September of 1905, this vivacious woman spent a lifetime learning how to live life to its fullest. The relevance of her ideas and practical advice on aging with vigor is convincingly shown by the fact that she finished the book at age 91, her spunk and enthusiasm undiminished over the years. "Remember, it's your body that's aging, not you!" she says. "I'd rather be over seventy than under fifty."

Rebecca, who has been married to her husband, Fred, for nearly seventy years, lives in Sonoma, California.